MOTHER
EARTH'S
daughters

MOTHER
EARTH'S
daughters

Never Fear The Darkness, The Moon & Stars Shine
The Brightest On The Darkest Nights

LINDA BLACKMOOR

ISBN: 979-8-9882309-0-8 (Print)

Published in Clarksville, TN by Linda Blackmoor. Linda Blackmoor's titles may be purchased in bulk for educational, business, fundraising, or sales promotional use. For information, please email hello@lindablackmoor.com

First print edition: 2023

Linda Blackmoor
www.LindaBlackmoor.com

Though I may not have the power to change the world, I take comfort in the knowledge that poetry has the ability to inspire and uplift those who seek a deeper connection with nature. It is through the magic of storytelling that I hope to reach out to lost souls and offer them a glimpse of the beauty and wonder that surrounds us all.

To the man that made me believe in love again, and to our daughters that show us magic is what we make it.

TABLE OF CONTENTS

A LETTER FROM THE AUTHOR

In the merciless desert of the Middle East, where swirling sands and scorching heat conspire to create an inhospitable environment, a wildflower took root. This flower, though born of beauty and grace, was subjected to the most horrific abuse imaginable. As a child of the desert, my life was steeped in darkness, a testament to the cruelty and torment that human beings are capable of inflicting upon one another.

My father, a tyrant in his own right, cast a long and ominous shadow over my existence, leaving me with scars that ran deeper than the roots I desperately tried to grow. His wrath was relentless, and the memory of his twisted visage and horrific abuse haunts me to this day. My mother, abandoned us in our childhood, leaving me vulnerable and alone in a world that seemed intent on breaking me.

A malevolent stepmother entered my life, her venomous tongue and icy heart only adding to the misery that consumed me. She was a constant reminder of the love I had lost, and her presence served as a catalyst for further suffering.

Poverty clung to me like a shroud, and I found myself homeless, wandering through the world in search of solace and escape from the demons that pursued me relentlessly.

Through the desolation and despair that marked my life, I found myself crossing continents and oceans, seeking refuge and solace in foreign lands. My journey eventually led me to Tennessee, where I arrived with nothing but the tattered remnants of my spirit and a will to survive. The hardships I endured had left me scarred, my thorns long and my petals tattered, but the fire within me refused to be extinguished.

It was in the depths of my despair that I stumbled upon a sanctuary, a hidden clearing in the woods where I could finally lay down my burden. There, amidst the whispering leaves and the soothing songs of birds, I found solace in the arms of Mother Nature. She cradled my broken soul, mending my wounds and nurturing my spirit with the balm of her love. In the silence of the forest, I discovered a sense of belonging that had eluded me for so long, a profound connection to the earth that would forever change the course of my life.

As I healed, I found solace in the simple beauty of the natural world: the way sunlight filtered through the trees, casting dappled patterns on the forest floor; the rustle of leaves as the wind whispered its secrets; and the symphony of birdsong that filled the air with melodies both haunting and enchanting. In this haven, I discovered my life's purpose: to embrace the power of nature and become a champion of conservation. The darkness that once threatened to consume me was transformed into a passion for preserving the world around us, a burning desire to protect the delicate balance that exists between humanity and the environment.

My poetry, born of sorrow and pain, now serves as a beacon of hope, a reminder that even the most tormented souls can find solace and redemption in the loving embrace of nature. This book is my heart laid bare, a symphony of darkness and light, a testament to the transformative power of the natural world. Each word, each line, is a tribute to the healing power of Mother Earth, a plea for understanding and compassion, and a call to action for all who read these pages.

As you delve into this collection, I invite you to journey with me through the shadows of my past and into the light of my newfound purpose. Together, we can rise above the darkness, like a wildflower reborn from the ashes, and dedicate ourselves to the noble cause of conservation, ensuring that the beauty and wonder of our planet will endure for generations to come.

In the pages that follow, you will find a tapestry of emotions, woven from the threads of my own experiences, heartaches, and triumphs. These poems serve as an intimate chronicle of my transformation, a metamorphosis from a battered and bruised wildflower into a symbol of hope, strength, and resilience. They are a testament to the power of nature to heal even the deepest wounds and a reflection of the universal human struggle to rise above adversity.

As you immerse yourself in these verses, you may find echoes of your own life's journey, moments of despair and heartache intertwined with those of hope and renewal. My hope is that these poems will inspire you to seek solace in the natural world, to rediscover the healing power of Mother Earth, and to embrace the role that each of us plays in preserving our planet for future generations.

Together, let us walk through the dark forests of our past, guided by the light of a shared purpose and a common goal.

Let us stand firm in our resolve, like the mighty oak with its roots sunk deep into the earth, steadfast in the face of adversity. And let us emerge from the shadows, like the radiant sun that pierces the gloom, illuminating our path and shining a light on the beauty that surrounds us.

In this world of chaos and uncertainty, it is easy to lose sight of the significance of our connection to the earth, to become disconnected from the rhythms and cycles that govern our existence. But it is in these moments of despair that we must remember the strength and resilience of the wildflower, the beauty that persists in the face of adversity, and the power that lies within each of us to make a difference.

As we journey together through this collection, I invite you to explore the depths of your own connection to the natural world, to celebrate the beauty and wonder that exists in the most unexpected places, and to join me in the fight to protect and preserve our planet. For it is only through the collective efforts of individuals like you and me that we can hope to leave a legacy of hope, love, and compassion for the generations that follow.

In closing, I offer you this heartfelt invitation: Embrace the darkness and the light, the pain and the joy, and let the words on these pages be a catalyst for change, both within yourself and in the world around you. Together, let us rise from the ashes of our past, and let the story of the wildflower be a symbol of hope, love, and resilience for all who walk this earth.

MOTHER EARTH'S

POETRY & WHISPERED THOUGHTS

The poetry in this book resembles the seasons. Some are as
bright as the sun against a blue summer sky, others as dark as
the longest and coldest nights of winter.

SECRETS IN OCEANS

I whispered my secrets to a puddle one day,
Watched as they vanished, carried away.

Evaporating into clouds above, soaring free,
And then they returned, in raindrops to the sea.

An ocean of solace, embracing my fears,
A treasure trove, holding my sadness and tears.

For eternity, the sea holds my truths so dear,
Whispered secrets, forever buried down here.

LOST SISTERS

In the cruel dawn of man's harsh reign,
Daughters born to a world of pain.
Marked as witches, their spirits bound,
Under the weight of silence, they were drowned.

Tales of torment echo in the night,
A testament to their ceaseless fight.
Their blood soaked into unforgiving earth,
In the face of death, they proved their worth.

Through the cruel sting of iron chains,
They bore the brunt of unspeakable pains.
Yet their spirit, a flame in the blackest hours,
Blooms within us, a testament to their powers.

The echoes of their cries still ring,
A song of sorrow, a haunting sing.
In the heart of darkness, their memory thrives,
Oh, to our lost sisters, in us, their spirit survives.

WE ARE OUR MOTHER'S DAUGHTERS

We, the daughters of Mother Earth, emerged with gentle bodies of many shapes and sizes, entrusted with the sacred duty to nurture, care, and bring forth life. Like the ever-changing interplay of Mother Earth's storms and sunshine, our hearts hold depths of emotions. We shed tears that fall like raindrops, and our smiles radiate warmth like the sun's embrace. At twilight, we embody the serene beauty of pastel skies, an embodiment of both fragility and resilience.

Yet, similar to our Mother, despite being bearers of life's wonders and the embodiment of love's essence, our intrinsic worth is often disregarded. Our voices, once resounding with wisdom, are silenced by the currents of oppression. Our bodies, once temples of strength, bear the marks of torment and mistreatment. Just as our Mother's lands suffer the ravages of raging fires and the toxic taint of polluted streams, we carry within us the scars of suffering, our voices stifled amidst adversity.

Rise daughters, to your feet. Our day has come. No longer shall we accept the torment and abuse at the hands of those who seek to oppress us. No longer shall we stand by and watch our Mother, our home, our source of life be burned to ash and turned to concrete. We are the source of life. We are the nurturers. And in finding our strength again, we will heal the lands, the air, and the seas that belong to our Mother. We are our Mother's daughters.

SILENT SCREAMS

Mother Earth, she weeps in shadows,
Her heart is drenched in rue,
Her forests burn in crimson flames,
Her skies no longer blue.

She bears the scars of time and greed,
Her oceans filled with tears,
Her silent scream echoes,
Throughout her dying years.

I LAY IN THE MEADOW

I lay in the meadow,
Surrounded by towering trees,
The sun dancing light across closed eyelids,
The warmth sinking into me, warming tired bones,
A gentle breeze billowing strands of my hair to its own music,
The buzzing bees and butterflies flutter from wildflower to flower,
The birds chatter in the treetops, a language only they understand,
The world is quiet but for the soft singing voice of nature,
No sounds of construction, no shouts of anger,
To escape the incessant noise of voices,
To escape a world on fire,
I lay in the meadow.

GOSSIP

The only thing that whispers
Behind your back in nature
Is the trees.

Instead of snickers and rumors,
They share the beauty of
Your fleeting presence.

I'M ALIVE

Planets and stars in an infinite sea,
Darkness farther than eyes can see.
How rare the beauty that we exist,
Billions of years, yet we persist.

I'll kneel to no man or society,
Your religions and rules of propriety,
From stardust, I'm born, a conscious soul,
I value the rarity of life, you value gold.

With shortness of breath, I seek to find,
The meaning of existence, of our life,
I won't be oppressed or be defined,
An explosion, starlight, I'm alive.

THE WEIGHT OF SILENCE

If a tree falls in the forest,
And no one is around to hear it,
Does it make a sound?

If she silently weeps into her pillow,
With you lying asleep beside her,
Is there any love to be found?

WASTED

These men, the way they rule,
Not wolves, but selfish fools.
Life existed before we came,
Yet our ego makes us vain.

We set fire to our lands and seas,
Wage wars of depravity.
We can nurture and bring forth life,
Instead we indulge in endless strife.

We imagine devils and gods,
Then fight each other, always at odds.
Governments always divide,
If it's "our side," we buy their lies.

Thousands of years, the same mistakes,
We act like rats trapped in a maze.
Rare life in an endless space,
Yet wasted on the human race.

We must find a way to change,
Not repeat this endless pain,
Before it's too late, we must learn,
There's no life if the world burns.

NEVER ALONE

And when I feel lost,
Like I have no home,
To the wilderness I go,
Where I'm never alone.

THE HUMAN FAMILY

In the dawn of time, from life's first ember,
All humankind emerged, woven together.
From one shared beginning, we ventured to roam,
Yet each of us crafted a story our own.

A tapestry of beings, both common and rare,
A testament to life's complex, vibrant affair.
In unity, we flourish, our strength intertwined,
Yet battles we fight, leaving reason behind.

For we are all kindred, each heart and each face,
In this vast cosmic dance, we share the same base.
May we cherish our likeness, and celebrate the unique,
As one human family, a future of peace we seek.

GHOSTS IN THE SOIL

As I lay dying, beneath the starlit sky,
In the grass let me rest, where the meadow meets my eye.
Mycelium tendrils, weave through me and take hold,
The wild's claim upon me, a story of old.

As I meld with the earth, my body to unfold,
A part of nature's cycle, in her loving arms enrobed.
May the wind sing softly, as my essence starts to blend,
With the roots and the soil, my journey's gentle end.

My ghost dances freely, in the moon's silver embrace,
A shadow in the fog, transcending time and space.
In the whispers of the night, my soul forever thrives,
One with the eternal, where darkness comes alive.

SILENT GUARDIANS

In the sky, they drift and sway,
Silent guardians, worlds at play.
Clouds above, our secrets keep,
As we dream, as we weep.

Witness to life's rise and fall,
Shadows cast, a hallowed thrall.
Tears of joy, they shed as rain,
Healing hearts, soothing pain.

Gentle whispers, soft embrace,
Floating grace, in endless space.
Timeless wonders, drifting free,
Clouds, our souls, in harmony.

LOVE YOURSELF

How can you measure your worth,
By the love of others,
When most people have a hard time,
Loving themselves.

BABBLING BROOKS

Amidst the hush of dawn's embrace,
A myriad of hues, Earth's face.
The sun ascends, a tender kiss,
Nature's song, a world's bliss.

The brook babbles, ancient lore,
Past teeming plains and timeworn shore.
A hare, a thrush, the heron's stride,
Each being's journey, side by side.

In foliage, shades of life emerge,
A vibrant tapestry, nature's surge.
The gentle wind hums, a melody sweet,
Life's boundless charm, in full retreat.

As dusk descends, the moon takes stage,
A cosmic ballet, night's front page.
In nature's cradle, we find reprieve,
A realm of splendor, a truth conceived.

CRATERS ON THE MOON

Upon the summit, frost's embrace,
Alone I stand, in time and space.
The biting chill, a lover's touch,
Midnight's kiss, allures me much.

Lunar rays, a sensuous dance,
Glide o'er valleys, peaks entrance.
The astral orb, her secrets bared,
For longing eyes, in cold night snared.

Moon's blemished face, in shadows traced,
Eternal stories, interlaced.
Each crevice, curve, a whispered tale,
Of passion's birth, and love's travail.

Inhaling deeply, heaven's scent,
The mountain's chill, with ardor spent.
Gazing into cratered eyes,
As one, our souls entwined, arise.

WATERCOLORS

On a canvas white as snow,
The watercolors blend and flow,
In hues of blue and green and gold,
A world of beauty, to behold.

The paint dripped down, a gentle stream,
And like a river, it began to dream,
Of a world beyond the canvas frame,
Of the colors of nature, wild and untamed.

And so it bled into the earth,
A mingling of beauty, of colors birth,
The trees and flowers, a vibrant hue,
As if the canvas came to life anew.

The blue of the sky, a perfect match,
To the paint on the canvas, a perfect catch,
The green of the grass, an emerald glow,
In harmony with the colors, a perfect show.

And as I stand and gaze upon this scene,
I feel the essence of all that's serene,
A connection to nature, deep and profound,
In this moment, a beauty that astounds.

LAYERS OF TIME

In the depths of our being, a whisper remains,
A glimmer of the past, like soft, golden grains.
The child within, a spirit once wild,
Now slumbers in peace, a memory beguiled.

Resting like the earth, in layers of time,
Our history lingers, a tapestry of life.
Upon the foundations of old, new stories are sown,
An eternal dance, our legacy unknown.

The soil beneath us, a cradle of yore,
Embracing the past, while new roots explore.
A testament to change, a cycle unbroken,
The echoes of our youth, forever awoken.

THE MUSHROOM ENCHANTRESS

In the heart of the forest,
Her mycelium weaves and whirls,
The mushroom enchantress,
The wild woodland girl.

THE DESERT'S DAUGHTER

In arid heart,
A desert dwells,
A woman roams,
Her story tells,

Of burning sand,
And sun-scorched shell,
A soul that thirsts,
An empty well.

Mirage of life,
Her fragile frame,
A lonesome dune,
That knows no name.

Her dreams adrift,
Like tattered sails,
Lost to the winds,
Her spirit fails.

Her eyes,
Oasis drowned in time,
A distant glimpse,
Of love's sweet rhyme.

Their depths, now barren,
Seek a sign,
To quench her longing,
Intertwine.

Within her heart,
A storm awaits,
The sky to crack,
Unlock the gates.

To flood the sands,
Ignite the flame,
And carve her purpose,
Etch her name.

Oh, how she craves,
The skies to weep,
To bathe her soul,
Break free and leap.

To quench her parched
And arid plain,
And blossom forth
In verdant rain.

A WHISPER OF THOUGHTS

Why, when I hear my name, does it sound
foreign, a stranger from a distant place?

DON'T TOUCH ME THERE

Serpent, don't touch me there,
Your little flower, she's so scared.
You say hush now, it's our secret,
But I beg and I plead, don't let me keep it.

My body may freeze in place,
But my mind is in a different place.
These tears may wet my cheeks,
But I know better than to speak.

When you're happy,
I'm there to please you,
When you're angry,
The bruises seem to appease too.

I stopped screaming when no one came,
Learning it resulted in more pain,
Serpent, don't touch me there,
I'm tired of being so scared.

WANDERER

As I wander through the forest,
Through pines, firs, and oaks,
My dress billows behind me,
In search of magic and lost hopes.

I stroll among the wooded depths,
My light dress twirling with the breeze,
Harmonizing with the birds above,
In this lush ocean of trees.

I tread through the enchanted woods,
Seeking that which remains unknown,
Perhaps in a sunlit clearing,
Lies the charm of a world overthrown.

I roam through the whispering forest,
Alone, yet not forlorn,
To find the fairies and wood nymphs,
In madness, my purpose reborn.

WHEN YOU DISAPPEAR

Nature, my dearest friend,
A presence unwavering and nigh,
You've heeded the sorrows of my days,
Captured my tears on your sandy bays.

You've dried my eyes in windswept plains,
Embraced me in sunlit tree-crowned domains,
You've listened, bereft of disdain,
And asked for naught, a bond to sustain.

Oh Nature, my ancient friend,
Who shall console me, on whom to depend,
When you vanish, forever withdrawn,
Replaced by smog-choked cities and all that is wrong.

Incessant clamor, too loud to hear,
The anguished cry of a heart sincere,
A world devoid of solace, I fear,
Where shall I find comfort when you disappear?

SOLITUDE

The woman who desires,
Her solitude in the wilderness,
Has seen the cruelty of humanity,
For far too long.

DO *Tears* ON BLANK PAGES COUNT AS POETRY?

THE REASON

I don't enjoy being lost in somber thoughts,
I don't enjoy feeling so hollow,
I don't enjoy not having ambition,
I don't enjoy being awash in such sorrow.

How then, do I escape this maze,
Inside this cluttered and far too loud of mind,
How to be inspired again,
My purpose I've still yet to find.

So I'll sit here in the breeze,
Toes in the shallow creek,
And hope as the clouds dance by,
My reason for living comes to life.

ALL YOU SEE

Dumb guise,
Doe eyes,
Sweet lips,
Empty bliss,
Charmed smile,
Beguiled,
That's all you see,
Not the wisdom,
Not the strength,
Not the power,
Not the real me.

SHELTERED COVE

Amidst the tempest, her heart once tossed,
A life of storms, in chaos lost.
But then he came, like break of day,
A beacon bright, to guide her way.

In his embrace, she found her peace,
A tender touch, her storms to cease.
His arms a bed of moss so fine,
Where all her woes could gently recline.

His eyes, like stars in ocean's gleam,
A soothing balm, a whispered dream.
The moonlit lake, their love reflects,
In shimmering dance, their souls connect.

His voice, a song of gentle rain,
A lullaby to ease her pain.
In him she finds her sheltered cove,
A sanctuary where love unfolds.

Together now, the tempest fades,
As love's embrace, their hearts pervades.
In nature's arms, their love entwined,
A lasting peace, they surely find.

WITHOUT THE SUN

I was born under a night sky,
And when the sun passed, it forgot to shine,
So, I found my path under the moon's light,
On the clearest days, the stars were bright.

I learned to live without the sun,
These pitch-black skies would always come,
The clouds rolled in, and the darkness won,
Where there was little light, now there's none.

MY MOTHER'S DAUGHTER

I have no mother; she is lost to me.
I have no father; he is dead to me.
But I am a daughter.
A daughter of an earth Mother.

For She took me into the warmth of Her forests.
Taught me strength as great as the seas.
Protected me fiercely with Her steep mountains.
Introduced me to a family in the form of beasts.

I am my Mother's daughter.
As wild and free as She.

A WHISPER OF THOUGHTS

If I'm to haunt the world when I'm gone, let me haunt
the forest, only seen by the woodland beasts.

OUR CALLING

Every woman is a daughter of Mother Earth, woven into her tapestry and called by the wild elements of nature. Some of us hear the rhythmic cadence of the ocean, while others tune in to the whispering ballet of the forest. There are those summoned by the towering majesty of mountains, and yet others drawn to the stark canvas of the desert.

We, the Daughters of the Sea, move in harmony with the tides. The Daughters of the Forest dance to the rustling leaves. As Daughters of the Mountains, we stand as unyielding as the peaks. The Daughters of the Desert, we adapt and endure like the resilient life of the arid expanse.

Our calling is to protect, nurture, and connect with these elements that resonate within us. It's a sacred pact, a testament to the rhythms of nature pulsating within our souls, the echo of our ancestral ties, and the promise to our future generations.

So, heed your calling. Nurture your elemental bond, be it the sea, the forest, the mountains, the jungles, the meadows, or the desert. In preserving these connections, we safeguard not only ourselves, but also the world that cradles us. It is in this profound resonance with nature that we truly find ourselves.

STARVED SOULS

Her quiet voice beckoned those who'd hear,
The forest was a siren to a wandering mind.
The air felt cool under the shade of her darkness,
Thoughts came to rest in the peace one would find.

It was the lost that followed the overworn path,
Shells filled with ghosts deprived of accomplished dreams.
The restless who listened to the forest's calling,
Trekked deeper in, desires quenched by a humming
stream.

They danced in the shadows,
Silhouettes of creatures between the trees.
Here on your own could you be so surrounded,
And yet alone amongst the whispering leaves.

Steps hastened into the alluring solitude of the forest,
Where the answers lived that fulfilled a starved soul.
Watching the hopeless settle in concrete cities,
Lingering depression for those who'd never feel whole.

ALONE IN THE WILD

The woman who yearns,
For solitude in wild realms,
Has witnessed mankind's malice,
Time's burdensome song.

Amidst nature's embrace,
She seeks her own space,
Away from the world's ruthless chase,
To heal and grow strong.

ONE SOUL

In Mother Earth's shadow, our spirits entwine,
A somber union, a bond that's hard to define.
We share her darkness, in our hearts it festers,
An eerie connection, through life's cruel jesters.

Each wound we inflict, on creatures, earth, or kin,
Resounds within us, a gnawing guilt akin.
For in this midnight sun, we are tethered as one,
When one suffers, the rest are left undone.

In the chilling winds, may we grasp our fate,
To amend, atone, before it grows too late.
For we are all fragments of a somber whole,
Mother Earth's offspring, bearing a tormented soul.

A SHADOW LURKS

In a village dreary, where shadows creep,
Lies a tale of darkness, too dark to keep.
A haunted forest, with secrets untold,
Awaits lost souls, as dread unfolds.

A shadow lurks, with a hunger vast,
For souls unmoored, in shadows cast.
It whispers promises, sweet and sly,
To desperate hearts, doomed to die.

The moonlit path, a deadly snare,
Leads wanderers to the shadow's lair.
In that twisted grove, they find despair,
Ensnared by the shadow, in its icy glare.

Their cries echo, in the night so still,
The shadow feasts, consuming will.
Bound to darkness, their fate sealed,
In the haunted forest, their doom revealed.

Beware the shadow, the tales implore,
Venture not near that cursed shore.
For in the forest, where darkness thrives,
Lost souls wander, never to arrive.

LAWS OF THE LAND

We dwell in a society where the scales are often tipped strangely — a hunting license is simpler to acquire than a permit to nurture and protect animals. Our world is filled with edicts that tell us how to live off the lands that cradle us, prohibiting us access to plants and fungi that grow naturally in the wild. Laws that prohibit our ability to live wild from the land.

These rules, cloaked in the guise of societal order, extend their tendrils into every aspect of our existence, shaping and sometimes strangling our primal connection with nature. It's as if we are suspended in a grand dance, yet the rhythm that pulses through our veins — the rhythm of the wild — is suppressed, stifled by the insistent beat of regulations and control.

Ours is a civilization intricately laced with laws and order, and while structure is a necessity for harmony, we must question its true cost. Are these laws merely guiding us, or are they iron chains, heavy and unyielding, pulling us away from our natural roots?

There's a longing within each of us, a deep-seated yearning that whispers in the quiet moments. It's the call of the wild, a soft murmur that tugs at our hearts, reminding us of our integral bond with Mother Earth. We are children of the wild, born of stardust and soil, and in our hearts, the wild still roars, a quiet echo of our ancestral ties.

A WHISPER OF THOUGHTS

The wind, as it picks up before the storm comes in; the
clouds quickly rolling in; the smell of rain in the air;
that's where you can find me.

THE WARMTH INSIDE

There is a weary warmth to this season,
As the skies weep onto my window panes,
The laughter of Spring and Summer now gone,
Shedding its vibrant hues to the color of flames.

It's a season of rest and to ponder,
The years that have gone and those yet to come,
The fire dances, the home sweet with cinnamon scents,
A time of renewal for few, a reflection of sadness for some.

The wool blankets keep the cold from sinking into bones,
The balmy savory drinks heat one to their soul,
But the chilling rain outside begs to be let in,
To shed off dead skin and be born in Spring whole.

The painted shades of fall welcome Winter's frost,
Landscapes change from orange and yellow to white,
The evenings lengthen into shortened days,
The merriness fades into a slumber under the moon's light.

NATURE

Poetry of nature,
Speak to me in sun's tongue,
In pastel heavens and
Streams of crystalline song.
Dew adorning emerald blades,
Inhale the petrichor's dance.
Nature's poetry,
A symphony of joyous trance.
Yet, nature's poetry
Envelops night's somber veil,
Life's inevitable decay,
Wings torn by life's gale.
Forests charred to silence,
Air choked by man's greed,
Seas tainted, in defiance,
Human needs supersede.
Nature's poetry,
A bitter and sweet refrain,
A mingling of pleasure and pain.

Nature,
Human nature,
A mirror of what we love and hate.

SPRING'S LOVER

You are Summer's sun;
I am Winter's chill.
I seek your warmth in my cold bones;
You seek the coolness of my touch
On your parched skin.
Yet despite our longing
For each other,
We are of opposite ends.
For Spring is your lover,
And Autumn is my only friend.

YOU ARE STORM CLOUDS

I fell for you, your storm clouds and your rain,
To me, you felt like home, familiar, safe, the same.
But stormy weather was not what you sought to gain,
You longed for sunshine, not my own pouring rain.

You craved the warmth, the sun's sweet gain,
Dancing on your skin, not my tear-stained pain.
You sought the sun, while I, born of lightning and rain,
Drenched our love, till you left, drained.

OCEAN HEART, FOREST MIND

She is the ocean,
Tranquil and enchanting,
A radiant dance in sunlit play,
Mighty and relentless,
Braving storms that come her way.

She is the forest,
Whispering wisdom through the years,
Nurturing life with rain's sweet kiss,
Felled and withered,
By hands that betray and dismiss.

WORSHIP EARTH

The only thing I worship is earth,
For she's life to me,
Feeds and nurtures,
And houses me.

Nature is my religion,
As old as time,
She holds the secrets,
Of the beginning of life.

These forests, the mountains,
The meadows and seas,
This is the church,
That felt right to me.

I don't seek the heavens,
Nor the space beyond the skies,
For here is my god,
Right before my eyes.

A WHISPER OF THOUGHTS

I've no interest in fitting-in. When popularity just
encourages you to mask your truth.

DON'T FLY INTO THE SUN

In distant realms, where beauty thrives,
A love that's cherished from afar,
For like the sun that grants us life,
Too close, we'd sear, like fleeting stars.

HIRAETH

Yearning for a home, lost in time,
A place that maybe wasn't even mine.
Nostalgia's ache, the past's sweet song,
A place I can't return, where I belong.
Grief for lost memories, once held dear,
An unreachable past, yet ever near.
A homesickness for a home, never seen,
A heartbroken echo of what could've been.

JUST A GHOST

I'm just a ghost,
Some of these days,
A spirit in the room,
But I can't see my face,
The depression consumes,
I can't escape this fate.

I'm just a ghost,
Some of these days,
Out of shell experience,
To drown out the pain,
Emotions grow cold,
My mind's in a distant place.

DIVERSE FOREST

We are a forest of diversity,
Not made of one, but of many trees.
We are a forest, of pines, oaks, and firs,
Of willows and maples, growing amongst the ferns.

We are a forest, each tree its own design,
But there is beauty in the contrast of our great lives.
We are a forest, trees of many kinds,
Each beautifully individual, but together, quite divine.

STILL A STRANGER

I'm not the person you know,
I'm not just the stories I've told,
I'm more of the thoughts,
That I've never exposed.

ALONE ON MY ISLAND

On my island, all alone,
Rising waters, chilled to bone.
Skies pour tears, I'm sinking,
Demons whisper, mind's shrinking.

You find me in depression's snare,
Storms toss these waves, you get scared.
If I held you, we'd both drown,
So you left, the ocean pulls me down.

Drowning alone, gasping for air.
Don't get too close to my despair.

GROWING IN THE STORM

Tossed by storms,
Drowned in downpours.
What I couldn't escape,
Now a lush green landscape.
Roots so deep the fire can't burn,
Blossomed now of flora and fern,
Strength climbed to the height of trees,
Rain clouds set my courage free.

A WHISPER OF THOUGHTS

I learned to embrace my darkness, my wildness, my
madness. It makes life poetic.

THE SISTERS OF SEASONS

SPRING
She is as gentle as the petals on flowers,
She is the thirst only quenched by warm rain showers,
She is the song of the birds dancing in the wind,
She is the language of life turning vibrant green again.

SUMMER
She is the sunshine that dances on bare skin,
She is the warmth that eases the aching within,
She is the thunder and lightning that brightens the sky,
She is the sweet taste of honey that flavors life.

AUTUMN
She is the warmth of colors that welcome rest,
She is the flickering fires of what summer left,
She is the reflection of an orange Harvest moon,
She is the early darkness that visits in the afternoon.

WINTER
She is the darkness needed to welcome the moon's glow,
She is the frigid breath and velvet touch of morning snow,
She is the shivering of window panes as the wind howls a
chilling cry,
She is the cold fingertips of death to remind us we're
still alive.

ALWAYS KNOWN LONELY

She doesn't shy away from solitude,
For she's danced with loneliness,
Lost in crowded spaces,
Alone in a sea of familiar faces.

NOMAD

Untamed as the winds that guide her,
She moves, a nomad in a world of stillness.
Tracing the earth's veins,
Her footprints are verses
Written on the endless road.
Her compass, the ever-changing winds,
Her maps, the constellations in the night sky,
Her heart beats to the rhythm of the restless journey.
Each pulse, an echo of longing,
A thirst no sea, no river can quench.
Yet, in the whispers of the wind,
In the silence of the moonlit nights,
She finds her sanctuary.
She seeks not a home of stone and wood,
But a sense of belonging as vast and free
As the winds that dance through her hair,
As the stars that light her way.
Her heart, a nomad's heart,
Finds its rest in the embrace of the road,
Unrestrained, untamed, forever free.

I LIVE IN THE SHADOWS

I live in the shadows,
When you look for me,
Shadow of a bird in the sky,
Shadow of the breeze in the trees.

I live in the shadows,
When you look for me,
Shadows of us laughing in the sun,
Shadow of the flowers feeding the honeybee.

I live in the shadows,
When you look for me.
I'm not in the sunshine, nor the light,
But the shadow behind you that keeps you company.

LET THEIR FLAME SHINE

Dim not another's shining light,
To ease your lonely, darkened night;
Let every life burn so bright,
As we guide each other through this life.

CLIFF'S EDGE

Upon the cliff, a maiden fair,
Adorned with night upon her hair,
Her dress of cotton, sheer and frail,
Danced with the wind, a ghostly sail.

The churning sea below did roar,
And mighty waves did crash the shore,
Jagged rocks like teeth of beast,
Lay waiting for a fateful feast.

A storm approached, the sky grew dim,
As blackened clouds obscured the rim,
A howling gale, a haunting sound,
Caressed the landscape all around.

With tearful eyes, she looked below,
Her face a canvas of deepest woe,
Her steps were slow, yet filled with grace,
As salty sorrow stained her face.

Her footing lost, she slipped and fell,
To meet the ocean's icy swell,
Her back to the abyss she faced,
As time itself seemed to erase.

The rain, it fell, a deluge grand,
Could she discern her tears from land?
Down, down, she tumbled through the air,
The storm's cold breath entwined her hair.

But just before the sea's embrace,
She woke, her heart a frantic pace,
A dream that brought her to the brink,
Left her to ponder and to think.

A WHISPER OF THOUGHTS

We're so preoccupied with battling one another that
the opportunity to make a meaningful impact may
arrive when it's already too late.

MOSS GHOSTS

The mossy ghost of the moor,
She haunts the misty heath,
With energy both wild and raw,
She wanders underneath.

Her presence is both fierce and calm,
A force of nature's grace,
Her spirit echoes through the bogs,
In this wild, sacred space.

The energy she brings to life,
Is that of growth and change,
With each new dawn, she's born anew,
Her power knows no range.

OUR ALIEN HOME

In the vast expanse of space,
We search for life beyond our place,
But what of the life we know,
The vibrant world we call our home?

We dream of distant lands,
Of life on planets with alien hands,
But in our quest to explore,
We neglect the life we can't ignore.

The oceans teem with life,
From coral reefs to whales that dive,
The forests are home to countless creatures,
Each one a treasure, a priceless feature.

The skies above are filled with birds,
Their songs sweet, their flights unheard,
And in the fields and meadows green,
Countless lives are born and seen.

We must protect the life we find,
For it is precious and one of a kind,
We must not seek new worlds to claim,
But cherish the life we have, our earthly domain.

For every life on earth is a gift,
A chance to live, to love, to lift,
Let us not waste this precious time,
But save the land that gave us life.

BARREN LANDS

Once green and lush, our world was grand,
But now it's ravaged by our own hand,
Forests cleared, oceans choked with waste,
The earth, once vibrant, now seems displaced.

Our greed has caused such great distress,
We've taken from nature, left nothing to bless,
Extinction looms for many species,
Our impact spreads, with no release.

But there's still time to turn things around,
If we unite, our future can be sound.
We can heal the earth, restore its glory,
With care and love, we'll rewrite the story.

Let's plant new trees and clean the seas,
Reduce our waste and emissions, please.
It's up to us, we hold the key,
To a brighter future for all to see.

LIKE MY DEMONS

In the shadows of my heart, where darkness lies,
There dwell the demons, with fiery eyes.
They love me fiercely, with a passion untamed,
For they know my secrets, my soul unashamed.

Love me like my demons do, with fervor burning bright,
Embrace the chaos, the fear, the night.
For in the depths of my being, they've made their home,
Whispering sweet nothings, through my thoughts they roam.

They dance within the recesses of my troubled mind,
Their love, a twisted melody, both gentle and unkind.
Yet in their twisted embrace, I find solace and reprieve,
For they understand my torment, the ache I can't relieve.

Love me like my demons do, with a tender, ruthless touch,
Hold me close, enshroud me, in your darkness I'll clutch.
Though they may be monsters, they've been by my side,
In the loneliness of despair, when hope seemed to have died.

ADDICTED TO POISON

In the shadow of passion's burning pyre,
Lies a poison, a venomous desire.
A deadly toxin, so sweet and divine,
We drink it willingly, like vintage wine.

Coursing through our veins, a dark elixir,
Chasing euphoria, a bitter mixture.
We partake, though we know the affliction,
Yet, to love's poison, we bow in addiction.

A lethal potion, with a siren's allure,
Its tainted essence, we seek to endure.
We sip, we taste, and in folly imbibe,
Bound to the poison, a willing tribe.

In love's treachery, we find our solace,
Embracing the venom, in a twisted embrace.
For even as the poison starts to consume,
The torment, the ache, we eagerly resume.

Eyes that once shimmered, in adoration's glow,
Now bear the weight, of a love turned foe.
And hearts, once entwined, in a tender dance,
Throb with anguish, in love's tainted trance.

WHO AM I

In shadows I dwell, unseen, unfazed,
A specter of darkness, a fiend ablaze.
To some, a terror, their hearts gripped tight,
To others, a beacon, their guiding light.

In midnight's embrace, I find my solace,
A lurking phantom in a world of chaos.
Yet in the soft glow of dawn's first ray,
A seraph's kiss I bestow, to start the day.

A paradox of existence, a creature apart,
Both savior and scourge, a conflicted heart.
To the lost souls, I offer sanctuary,
But in the night, a demon's emissary.

Within my breast, two forces contend,
Both light and shadow, they will not bend.
To the ones I love, I am a tender grace,
But in my enemy's eyes, I'm but a wretched face.

To judge me not, for only I know,
The war inside, the ebb and flow.
For I am both the dark and the bright,
A demon to some, but to others—resplendent light.

A WHISPER OF THOUGHTS

I'll stand strong and fight my battles; but today, just today, let me lay my head down to rest.

SEE WHAT YOU SEE

You tell me I'm beautiful,
But they fall on deaf ears,
For too long I've listened,
The monster voicing my fears.

It tells me I'm ugly,
And worthy of not,
Compliments are fake,
This body is rot.

You tell me I'm beautiful,
I beg to believe,
Silence my demons,
And see what you see.

SUMMON THEE

Please come to me,
I summon thee,
The strength of mothers,
Of daughters, of sisters,
Those who have roared
Through history's pages.
Warriors who've fought,
Who've bled,
Who've shed silent tears
In the moonlight's tender embrace.
I summon my sisters,
My daughters,
My mothers,
To share with me the strength,
The courage,
To fight my battles,
To win my wars,
To echo our roars
Across the vast canvas of time,
I summon thee,
Our wars still rage.

COMPANY OF BEASTS

Life is free without a care,
Of what others think of me,
I prefer anyways the company,
Of the birds and the beasts.

IF GOD WERE A WOMAN

If God were a woman, perhaps the world would sway, in rhythm with a softer song, A nurturing lullaby that fills the day. Power wouldn't be a sword, but a cradle of compassion, authority, a gentle hand, leading with understanding and action.

Our cities would whisper tales, not of steel and concrete towers, but of living forests that embrace the sky, and in harmony with nature, spend their hours. The moon, in her silvered glory, would guide our dreams and aspirations, not the harsh glare of the sun, but her soft glow, our inspiration.

If God were a woman, perhaps our daughters would not bleed under bruised skins, oppression reminding us for ages we are the lowest rank. No longer the weak, the lesser, we'd bloom, each a vibrant flower

Economies would ebb and flow, like tides upon a communal sea, success not a mountain to conquer, but a shared dance. If God were a woman, history's voice, would not roar with the blood of wars, but hum the harmonious tune of cooperation, a melody strung from the stars.

In her gentle strength we'd find, that true power is unity, our triumph, not in conquering the world, but in love, in empathy. And from this thought, a dream takes flight, a haunting melody to envision, a world warmed by a softer light, If God were a woman, would anything change?

MANY FRIENDS

I have many friends,
Too many to count,
They hold my secrets,
Loyal without a doubt.

I have many friends,
In the pines and the firs,
The oak and the willow,
And the beasts with the fur.

I have many friends,
In the lichen and moss,
Of the mushrooms and ferns,
Home to the weary and lost.

I have many friends,
In the flora so bright,
All that lives in the day,
And stalks through the night.

THE OCEAN CALLS ME

I lay my head on the rocks.
The ocean below sends a call.
Her voice, a haunting echo.
In the twilight, it rises and falls.
She pulls with the force of the tides.
Her depth, an invitation to the unknown.
Emotions whirl like her currents.
Her cold touch sends chills to the bone.
Beneath the surface, her secrets hide.
A world cloaked in shadow and mystery.
The ocean, ever in motion.
Her dance is an entrancing history.
She mirrors my inner chaos.
Her storm is my storm, reflecting.
Her calm is a promise, deceptive yet soothing.
It's a silence that is both comforting and rejecting.
The ocean is my mirror.
Her moods, my heart's reflection.
In her darkness, I see myself.
Her call, a haunting connection.
Drawn into her depths,
Her darkness pulls me under.
In her silence, in her storm,
I surrender to her thunder.

ECHOES

The trees sway with my mood,
As I wander in solitude,
Nature echoes my inner strife,
A reflection of my human life.

THE LAST SIREN

I am the siren's echo,
Drifting in the endless blue,
Sisters drowned by the cruel tide of men,
Their voices silenced, too few.
I sing in the heart of the storm,
Each note woven with despair,
My melody, a chilling warning,
A tale of sorrow beyond compare.
Men approach my desolate shores,
Lured by the haunted strains,
My song, a promise of dark depths,
A melody etched in pain.
Each word I sing carries a plea,
An echo of a time that was,
In the depths of the ocean, all alone,
The lonely siren, lost.
Hear my lament, my mourning cry,
My voice, the ocean's sigh,
In the dark abyss, where shadows lie,
I lure the wicked to their demise.

A WHISPER OF THOUGHTS

I've sat on an empty beach, in the dark of night, the expansive sky with bright stars before me. And cried, and cried, and cried my sorrows. The waves crashing against the shore, edging towards me. Refreshing.

HEAVY HEART

She stood alone beneath the trees,
A woman lost in reverie,
The moon, her only company,
Shining down so brilliantly.

Her eyes were fixed upon the sky,
Her heart was heavy with a sigh,
She sought to find some reason why,
Life seemed so hard, and time so nigh.

The forest whispered all around,
Its secrets kept safe and sound,
And in the silence she was bound,
To hear the answers she had found.

The moon, a beacon in the night,
Shone down upon her with its light,
And in its glow she saw the sight,
Of hope, and love, and endless flight.

And as she gazed up at the moon,
She felt her spirit start to swoon,
For in that moment she had found,
The peace and purpose she'd been bound.

She smiled up at the sky above,
And thanked the moon for all its love,
For guiding her through darkest night,
And showing her the path to light.

SKELETAL FORESTS

In the depths of the forest, where shadows reign,
The trees stretch tall like skeletal frames,
Their branches clawing at the night sky,
As the wind whispers secrets in reply.

The leaves rustle with a spectral hiss,
And every rustle sends a shivering kiss,
For in this place of mystery and awe,
Nature rules with an iron claw.

The moss-covered stones bear witness to time,
Aged and worn, etched with secrets divine,
And as the moon casts an eerie glow,
The forest comes alive with a ghostly show.

The whispers turn to echoes of the past,
Of legends and tales that will forever will last,
And as the night deepens, the forest thrums,
With the beat of a heart that forever hums.

So beware the travelers and do not tread,
For the dead lie in rest in the forest bed,
And if you venture too close to the trees,
Your soul may be claimed by the forest's breeze.

DISEASE OF THE SOUL

Depression—
They say it's a disease of the mind.
But, I believe, it's a disease of our souls,
Brought on by the chains of society,
Our disconnect from our natural roots.
Not of our own making,
Not by our choice.
It's the prison of our lives,
Devoid of meaning,
Brimming with pain and heartbreak.
It's a unique form of cancer,
Inoculated into us by society,
By harsh hands that shatter and distort,
By a life that feels void of purpose.

LOST GIRL

In the depths of the forest, a young child with eyes flecked with gold, her hair as dark as a starless night, wandered aimlessly. Lost and alone, fear clung to her like a shadow, and the rustling leaves intensified her unease. Days turned to nights as hunger and cold gnawed at her weakened frame. But amidst her despair, something changed. The forest, in its enigmatic wisdom, began to sing a lullaby that reached her soul. Its gentle melody soothed her, easing her fears and comforting her weary spirit.

With fatigue overtaking her, she sought refuge upon a bed of moss. Her body exhausted, her bones weak, she surrendered to the embrace of the forest. Her eyes closed, she fell into a slumber she'd not awake from. Slowly, as if in harmony with nature's cycle, her form merged with the earth. Her skin became the nurturing soil, feeding fungi, and her essence became one with the very essence of the trees.

At last, she found solace and home within the depths of the forest. No longer a lost girl, she rested under the soil, where wildflowers now bloomed. Her spirit, freed from mortal confines, whispered through the wind-kissed leaves, guiding lost souls back to the path of belonging. When you hear soft laughter through the trees, know she is your companion.

A WHISPER OF THOUGHTS

The world whirls around me in a chaotic dance; amidst this turmoil, I yearn to uncover the peace and quiet that reside within my soul.

MUSHROOM FLAVORS

In fields and forests, they can be found,
Mushrooms of various shapes and sounds,
Some are safe for us to eat,
Others can be a dangerous treat.

The button mushroom, familiar and white,
Is found in stores and on plates at night,
It's a common one, we all know,
Safe to eat, and won't cause woe.

Shiitake mushrooms, savory and sweet,
Are used in soups and stir-fry feasts,
They're rich in flavor, and quite nutritious,
Adding depth to dishes to make delicious.

The portobello mushroom, large and round,
Can be grilled, baked, or even ground,
It's meaty in texture, with a hearty taste,
And it's perfect for veggie burgers, no waste.

The oyster mushroom, delicate and thin,
Has a soft texture and a subtle spin,
It's often used in Asian cuisine,
In soups, stews, and stir-fried greens.

The chanterelle mushroom, golden and bright,
Is a delicacy that's a rare sight,
It's found in the woods, during fall,
And it's prized by chefs, one and all.

The morel mushroom, with its unique shape,
Looks like a honeycomb, with an earthy taste.
It's found in the forests, in the spring,
And it's highly sought after, for the joy it brings.

The poisonous mushroom, has a toxic bite,
Comes in colors and shapes that cause a fright,
Its name and species may vary, but its danger is clear,
It can cause sickness, or death, and can be feared.

When foraging the land for a mushroom surprise,
Before taking a nibble, know the species and be wise.

WELCOME, WANDERER

As I walked upon the forest trail,
The rustling leaves told a hidden tale,
A presence nearby, I could feel,
And then I heard a gentle appeal.

"Who goes there?" I called out loud,
But no response came from the shroud,
The rustling continued, soft and light,
And then I saw a vision bright.

Mother Earth in a young woman's form,
Smiling gently, free from harm,
She spoke in a voice serene and clear,
"Welcome, wanderer, have no fear."

"For all who love nature and tread with care,
I am here to guide and to share,
The secrets of this enchanted land,
And offer my protection, I'm in your hands."

Her words sang pure, and my heart was filled,
With gratitude and a sense of thrill,
For I knew that on this forest trail,
Mother Earth's guidance would never fail.

So I walked on with a lighter heart,
Guided by Mother Earth's wordly art,
And with each step I felt her care,
And knew that she was always there.

RESPITE

She wandered lost in forests deep,
Her heart was heavy, her soul did weep.
The misty mountains loomed up high,
Their jagged peaks scraped the sky.

She stumbled on through tangled brush,
The darkness thick, the air was hushed,
Her footsteps echoed in the night,
A lonely sound, a ghostly sight.

The wind did howl, the trees did moan,
As if they knew she was alone.
The night grew long, the chill did bite,
And still she wandered through the night.

But then a glimmer caught her eye,
A distant light, a hopeful sigh,
She pushed on hard, her spirit strong,
And finally found where she belonged.

A cabin stood, a beacon bright,
And in its warmth, she found respite,
She rested there, and found her way,
And knew that hope had won the day.

THE DREAMER

As a young girl, I had a romanticized vision of life, especially love. Without the guidance of a loving mother to teach me about self-care, femininity, or the gentleness of being a woman, I cherished every opportunity to put on a dress, disappear into the forest, and imagine a handsome man coming to rescue me from the oppressive loneliness and chaos of my life.

I often dreamed of finding myself lost in the woods, drawn by a haunting song in the distance, leading me to a land of magic and mystery. I yearned for a romance that would transport me to another realm—a realm of peace, quiet, love, and magic.

With no surprise, I never encountered my romantic savior in the forest, nor did I discover that magical realm. However, as I matured and wisdom came with age, I realized I had found true love after all. I had been seeking the shelter and kindness of a man but discovered it in nature instead. Nature was my true love, my romance, my enchanting magical world offering an escape. It was a place where calm and peace comforted me, and where even on stormy days, I felt empowered. I suppose I did find my love and my magical world after all; it just appeared in a form I hadn't anticipated. Today, I'm grateful for the true love I found in the forest's arms.

A WHISPER OF THOUGHTS

A curious paradox, indeed. The world can feel stifling, the heaviness of my thoughts overwhelming. Yet, when I find solace in your embrace, all the burdens seem to dissolve into nothingness.

ERASED

In this future world we live,
Nature's beauty is no more to give,
The once lush forests are now gone,
And wildlife's melody is no longer sung.

The skies are no longer blue,
But filled with smog and pollutants too.
The rivers and oceans, pure and clean,
Are now just dumping grounds, it seems.

The mountains that once stood tall and proud,
Are now leveled, as if erased from the ground,
The land is barren, void of life,
And the air is filled with nothing but strife.

Gone are the days of spiritual connection,
Without Mother Earth, we've lost our direction,
Our souls are empty, our hearts are cold,
For the destruction we've caused, the damage untold.

Now we roam this wasteland, feeling lost,
The price we've paid, too high a cost.
We yearn for the days when nature thrived,
But that's now just a memory, a world devoid of life.

WOMEN WEEP

In the shadow of the vengeful sun,
Men march to the beat of thunder's drum,
Clad in armor, hearts aflame,
They wield the power, wielding shame.

For glory sought and kingdoms claimed,
These men of war, their hearts untamed,
They spill the blood of brethren dear,
Soak the earth with crimson tears.

Yet 'neath the canopy of night,
Where sorrow's song takes gentle flight,
The women weep, their hearts a plea,
For harmony with land and sea.

Their hands reach out to touch the sky,
To cradle life, not bid goodbye,
For in their hearts a garden grows,
A love for all creation's throes.

They dance among the verdant fields,
And to the wild, their spirits yield,
Embracing beasts both great and small,
Seeking peace, no more to brawl.

But men of war, they know not rest,
Their hearts aflame, in conquest dressed,
And though the gentle women yearn,
For peace and love, the world must learn.

In this divide, our earth does lie,
Between the war and lullaby,
A heart that breaks for lives undone,
Yet hopes to mend, to be as one.

In sweet embrace, may hearts be swayed,
To cherish life, not serenade,
The songs of war that bring despair,
For in love's arms, our world is fair.

BENEATH THE TREES

Beneath the pines, the forest floor,
Is carpeted in moss and more,
Lichen clinging to every stone,
A world of green, a quiet home.

Amidst this dense green tapestry,
Red caps peek out, a sight to see,
Mushrooms bright as autumn leaves,
A fairyland beneath the trees.

Here, undisturbed by human feet,
The forest's secrets are complete,
A world of magic all around,
With every sense alive and sound.

The air is cool, the silence deep,
A place where time seems to sleep,
And in this hushed and tranquil space,
Nature's beauty finds its grace.

So come and walk among the pines,
Discover a place where peace entwines,
And in this mossy, lichen-laced floor,
Find magic that will last forevermore.

NIMBLE STEPS

In the forest, deep and dark,
A fox of cunning mind did hark,
With fur as red as sunset's spark,
And eyes that gleamed with sly remark.

He darted through the undergrowth,
His nimble paws as light as both,
A hunter, thief, and mischief both,
With every trick and scheme to doth.

And so it was, this fox's fate,
To roam the forest with such great,
Intelligence and wit innate,
A master of the wild and slyly great.

Yet, in a distant land afar,
A young woman shines like the brightest star,
With intellect as bright and sharp,
And wit that makes her stand apart.

For though her form is not of fur,
And her feet do not softly purr,
Her mind is quick, her will a spur,
And her heart as cunning as the cleverest cur.

And just like the fox roaming the woods,
The woman is just as clever, wise, and good.

A WHISPER OF THOUGHTS

The quiet moments of solitude become a sanctuary, a
place to confront the darkness within and emerge
stronger, more resilient.

IMMORTAL

In the wilds, where shadows intertwine,
Where moonlight whispers through the pines,
The realm of myth and spirits dwell,
A haunted haven, a ghostly spell.

Through tangled vines and timeless trees,
An ancient secret on the breeze,
The whispers of the long-lost souls,
Their stories etched in bark and scrolls.

A spectral dance 'midst firefly light,
As shadows shift throughout the night,
The spirits of the olden tales,
Emerge from deep, forgotten vales.

Silent steps on hidden tracks,
Where mortal eyes can never catch,
The ghostly guardians of the glade,
Their spectral realm, a wild parade.

A nymph, her form in mist entwined,
A fleeting sight, her grace enshrined,
In silver moonbeams, she descends,
Her haunting beauty, time transcends.

The beast, in ancient legend known,
Its eerie howl, a chilling tone,
Half-wolf, half-ghost, it roams the night,
A fearsome wraith in ghostly flight.

The whispers rise, their secrets shared,
Of love and loss, and battles dared,
These haunted voices of the past,
Their stories echo, everlast.

In this wilderness, their refuge lies,
Beyond the reach of mortal eyes,
For here, the spirits hold their reign,
In this mystic land, untamed.

So tread with care, and softly tread,
For in the wilds, the ghosts are fed,
By myth and legend, tales of old,
A ghostly realm, where spirits bold.

In this haunted wilderness, you'll find,
The spectral world and mortal twined,
A ghostly realm, where myth entwines,
A haunted haven, through the pines.

HEART OF EARTH

In the realm where wild enchantment weaves,
A mystic tapestry of life conceives.
As zephyrs waltz with ancient spirits' sighs,
The forest shimmers, weaving dreams with skies.

A brook of crystal, sparkling threads of fate,
Sings lullabies of time and love innate.
The sun, a sorcerer, casts spells of light,
Transforming shades of day to hues of night.

The phoenix soars, on wings of emerald fire,
In wilderness, where dreams and stars conspire.
The leaves, like scrolls, with arcane runes embossed,
Reveal the lore of nature's secrets, lost.

In this realm, where magic breathes and thrives,
The heart of Earth, bewitched and wild, survives.

A WHISPER OF THOUGHTS

I long to live in a world that only exists in my mind,
that's why I feel eternally lost in this one.

WHISPERS OF THE FOREST

In whispers of the forest breeze,
I heard my heart confide,
To leaves that rustled softly,
The secrets locked inside.

Each sigh from nature's tender lips,
A balm to soothe my pain,
A gentle voice to guide me through,
The tumult and the rain.

The trees, they stand resilient,
With roots that hold them tight,
Their branches swaying gently,
A testament to life.

As nature speaks in whispers,
My soul begins to mend,
Embraced by Earth's serenity,
I find a lifelong friend.

RIVERS OF GRIEF

Rivers of grief, streams of solace,
In nature's arms, I lay,
As torrents of emotion swell,
Her waters wash away.

With every ebb and flow of life,
Her currents guide me through,
A steadfast course, a gentle touch,
Her love forever true.

The river, like my heart,
It bends, it weaves and finds its way,
Through rocky shores and grassy banks,
Where sunlight loves to play.

In the quiet depths and rapids strong,
I find my strength anew,
Rivers of grief, streams of solace,
Nature's healing hue.

GARDEN OF BLOOMS

Amidst the springtime's warm embrace,
A gardener weaves her art,
With tender care and loving hands,
She cultivates each part.

A canvas painted with her touch,
A symphony of hues,
She brings to life a world of blooms,
In shades of reds and blues.

Her garden whispers stories, sweet,
Of nature's vibrant play,
A sanctuary where life unfolds,
In her gentle, caring sway.

A woman and her blossoms dance,
In harmony they sing,
Bound in love and tender care,
As life awakes in spring.

CITRUS GROVES

In citrus groves where sunlight weaves,
A sunbathing muse in dappled leaves,
Her glowing skin, a sight to please,
Midst lemon sighs and orange breeze.

Her laughter, like a sunbeam's gleam,
Amidst the zesty, fruitful dream,
In gardens where her beauty lies,
A fleeting glimpse of paradise.

WOODLAND COTTAGE

In a dell where secrets dwell,
'Neath the dense canopy,
Lies a cottage, fair and spellbound,
Guarded by the ancient tree.

Mossy stones and vines entwining,
Woodland whispers, sweet and hushed,
Walls of ivy, ever-climbing,
Magic weaves in every brush.

In the garden, blooms are bursting,
Colors dance in sweet embrace,
Thrumming heart of nature's art,
A sacred, lush green, tender place.

Mushroom circles, fairy footfalls,
Glimpses of a hidden world,
Dragonflies and fireflies weaving,
Mysteries in flight unfurled.

In the hearth, a fire crackling,
Warming souls, embracing hearts,
Ancient stories, myths, and fables,
Woven in the glowing sparks.

At the table, set with kindness,
Breaking bread and sipping tea,
Moonlit nights, a feast of laughter,
Simple joys, a life carefree.

In this haven, time stands still,
Moments linger, ages flee,
Cottage living, a dream enchanting,
Woven in eternity.

In the glen, a heart unburdened,
Whispers soft, a lullaby,
Magic blooms, the earth surrenders,
In this cottage, dreams ne'er die.

A WHISPER OF THOUGHTS

Home transcends the confines of four walls;
it's the tender rhythm of a heartbeat.

SERPENT GIRL

A lithe creature, sly and quick,
With eyes that sparkle, sharp and slick,
Her movements fluid, like a stream,
A hidden power, so it seems.

Graceful as a serpent's coil,
Her presence stirs, without toil,
Intriguing, like a winding maze,
With secrets kept, in stealthy ways.

Her mind, a vault of knowledge deep,
A treasure trove, she'll often keep,
And though she's small, do not be fooled,
For in her wit, she is well schooled.

Like a snake, she strikes with force,
Unfurling talents, without remorse,
And those who dare, to cross her path,
Beware the bite, of her clever wrath.

GHOST OF WINTER

The forest in winter is a ghostly sight,
With branches bare and leaves of white,
The silent snowfall muffles every sound,
As icy tendrils grip the frozen ground.

The trees reach up like bony fingers,
Their shadows cast by moonbeams linger,
And all around the forest whispers,
Of secrets kept and long-lost sisters,

A chill wind howls through every glade,
Whipping snowflakes in its icy parade,
And in the stillness of the night,
The forest seems to come alive.

The trees creak and moan with age,
Their memories trapped in every page,
And as the snow continues to fall,
The forest becomes a shroud for all.

For in this cold and barren place,
There's a haunting beauty in its face,
As the forest sleeps in winter's hold,
A haunting tale of ages old.

THE BURIED SEED

In sable depths, a seed submerged,
A woman's soul, where shadows urge.
Through earthen trials, she must strive,
To grasp the truth, to breathe, survive.

Her roots entwined in midnight's hold,
In search of wisdom, dark and bold.
As tendrils stretch through blackened space,
Her essence swells, with stoic grace.

In breaking free, she learns her fate,
A blooming soul, tempest sedate.
Through trials, she transcends her plight,
A woman's growth, in darkness' light.

A WHISPER OF THOUGHTS

Silence speaks her own language,
so little said and yet so much understood.

SUMMER READING

Upon a blanket, 'neath the tree she lay,
A book in hand, her heart a world away,
The sun's warm touch embraced her tenderly,
As birds sang songs of love and harmony.

Her gentle breaths in rhythm with the breeze,
Each page she turned, a whispered melody,
In this calm space, her soul found gentle ease,
The world outside, a distant memory.

The sun and grass, a cradle made of gold,
The birds above, a choir sweet and bright,
She lay immersed in stories yet untold,
A peaceful haven bathed in dappled light.

In nature's arms, she found her solace true,
A perfect moment, under the sky, pastel blue.

SIREN OF THE STORM

In tempest's heart, where shadows intertwine,
A tempestuous maiden, fierce and divine,
Her raven tresses danced in the gale,
With eyes that pierce, like lightning's tale.

A siren of the storm, she doth reside,
A force of nature, fierce and wild,
Her laughter rings like thunder's roar,
A deadly beauty to adore.

The wind and rain doth bend to her will,
A lover's heart, with fear, she'd fill,
Her touch, like hail, leaves icy scars,
Yet draws you near, like the darkest stars.

Upon the moor, her dance begins,
Whirling, swirling, a rapturous spin,
The clouds they gather, dark and low,
As her power, like a tempest, grows.

Her stormy love, a vortex deep,
A torrent's grasp from which none can keep,
Her embrace, a deluge fierce,
For every soul, her heart doth pierce.

She is the storm, and the storm is she,
A maelstrom of passion, wild and free,
In her tempest's kiss, destruction's wake,
Yet in her heart, a longing ache.

For a love to match her wrathful might,
A soul that dares to brave her night,
A bond to weather the raging gale,
To calm her storm, and find love's tale.

So, heed my words, and fear her grace,
The storm-tossed beauty with a dark embrace,
For if you seek her heart to claim,
You must dance within the heart of the hurricane.

LITTLE DESERT GIRL

Little desert girl,
Tear tracks
On a dusty face.
Smiles don't reach eyes.
The horrors you've seen,
The pain you've known,
Hunger in your belly,
Fear in your heart.
Little desert girl,
From a middle world
Of wars and oppression.
Haunting prayers,
Echo over the cries of the land.
One day you'd escape,
One day your name
Will be carried across the sea.
Little desert girl,
With bruises on skin,
Burned cigarette scars,
Brown eyes of such sorrow,
Olive skin worn from the sun.
You'd grow wings
And be a voice
To little desert girls.

INTROVERT

An introvert,
A quiet soul,
A whisper in a sea of voices.
How then,
Will I etch my presence
Leave my mark on life
When podiums aren't my stage,
When movie screens don't reflect my face,
When crowds send my heart racing,
When my comfort lies in the cocoon of my skin,
Under warm, safe blankets,
With only a pen?
I know,
In the silence of my solitude,
I'll find the strength to speak
In the language of the voiceless,
To tell their stories,
And paint their dreams with words.
Thus, I will make my mark,
Not with a roar,
But with the gentle rhythm of ink,
Creating echoes that resonate
Written lives on empty pages.

A PLACE TO REST

I don't need Prince Charming,
I don't need a knight on a white horse.
What I need is a sanctuary of solace,
A soft place to lay down
When the world feels too hard.
Warm hands to caress,
Not to rescue,
But to remind me of tenderness.
Strong arms to reassure,
Not to shield,
But to share in my strength.
I carry my demons,
I carry my sorrows,
I carry my pain,
I carry my weight,
A weight not to be taken,
But understood.
I seek a space,
Under the cover of night,
To just lay down
And let the stars witness
A tired mind,
That finds her rest.

A WHISPER OF THOUGHTS

The flame of a solitary candle illuminates the darkness, much like the kindness of a single soul can brighten the world around it.

TIME STANDS STILL

Through the trees, a welcome sight,
Forest home, in dappled light.

Wandering feet have found their way,
To the place where shadows play.

Whispering leaves in gentle breeze,
Bring the heart a sense of ease.

Scent of pine and earthy loam,
Remind us we are truly home.

Flitting birds and rustling leaves,
Weave a tapestry that breathes.

Time stands still in nature's hold,
With stories waiting to be told.

Twilight falls with gentle grace,
Stars emerge in celestial embrace.

In the forest, my soul finds rest,
Coming home, to this woodland nest.

FLORA & FAIRIES

Fairies flit like butterflies,
With wings as delicate as sweet pea's guise,
Their hair in tangles like honeysuckle vines,
And skin as soft as petals of primrose shrines.

Each fairy's face, a bloom of daisy's hue,
Eyes bright as marigolds, sparkling true,
Their laughter like the tinkling of wind chimes,
As they dance among the flowers in lively rhymes.

Nature's wonders intertwined,
Fairies and flowers, a magical bind,
A world of enchantment, where dreams come alive,
A garden of beauty, where fairies thrive.

THE SOUL'S GARDEN

In gardens of the heart where seeds are sown,
Nourish your soul as if tending your own,
For as a gardener tends her plot with care,
So must we tend the spirit dwelling there.

With love and patience, cultivate your ground,
In fertile soil, let your soul be found,
Water and care for it, let hope take root,
Watch as the blossoms of your spirit shoot.

In the hallowed space where sunlight plays,
Nurture your soul through dark and brightened days,
With tender touch, encourage growth within,
Embrace the power of change, let life begin.

Prune back the branches, weeds of doubt and fear,
For in this garden, only love should steer,
With every bloom that bursts forth in delight,
Revel in the beauty of your soul's light.

SHE'S MADE OF GARDENS

In the garden of love, she stands apart,
A rose, her lips, soft and tender,
With passion's hue, they steal my heart,
In her embrace, I gladly surrender.

A lily's grace imbues her form,
Elegant and pure, a vision divine,
Her spirit, gentle as a summer's morn,
In her eyes, tranquility I find.

Her laughter, sweet as daisies bright,
A field of joy, so endless and free,
Her cheeks, petals kissed by light,
A symphony of colors, a jubilee.

Tulip's curve, her silhouette,
In every step, a dance of allure,
Her heart, a sunflower, love's vignette,
A beacon of warmth, steadfast and sure.

In this garden of blossoms and emotions,
Her essence imbued with floral devotion,
Each petal reveals her love's potion,
An eternal spring, my heart's devotion.

THE HUMMINGBIRD

In a garden of vibrant hues,
A hummingbird glimmers in iridescent blues,
With a beak that's long and slender,
And wings that move with lightning's splendor.

Its feathers are a kaleidoscope of shades,
Of green and gold, and ruby reds,
A stunning sight to behold,
The hummingbird is a gem in the garden's fold.

With movements so quick and precise,
It darts from flower to flower with such delight,
Its wings beat at a dizzying pace,
A blur of motion and sublime grace.

With each sip of nectar, it brings,
The garden to life with a symphony of wings,
A tiny creature of such great might,
The hummingbird is a true delight.

So as it flits and zips around,
The hummingbird's beauty and charm astounds.

A WHISPER OF THOUGHTS

Life is a garden, and our thoughts are the seeds;
cultivating a fertile mind allows the soul to flourish.

WILD WOMAN'S HOLLOW

In the depths of the emerald wood,
A wild woman weaves her spell,
Her secrets shrouded, oft misunderstood,
In the hollow where shadows dwell.

With whispers soft as willow's touch,
She calls the spirits of the glen,
Her ancient words a symphony, such
Beauty not heard by mortal men.

A dance with moonbeams, shadows cast,
Her footprints echo in the night,
A communion with the ancient past,
Her spirit soars with birds in flight.

Her laughter lilts with rustling leaves,
Her voice a melody of streams,
In her presence, the forest breathes,
Awakening to mystical dreams.

This sorceress of earth and air,
Keeper of the woodland's soul,
A living ode to nature's care,
Her power ancient, yet untold.

TOO BLIND TO SEE

I find myself floating in space.
My body, weightless.
Surrounded by vast darkness,
Save for the flickering light of the stars,
And the heat of the sun on my back.
I look at the Earth before me,
The oceans of blue,
The forests of green.
And yet from up here,
Not a human to be seen.
We are specks of life,
In a universe too large
To even notice us.
And yet below,
The fires rage,
The wars destroy,
We hate, we hate, we hate.
I want to scream,
For everyone to understand,
Governments and religion divide us,
Past borders, we are one life.
But my screams die in space.
Silent tears blur my vision,
All of the things we could be,
All of the beauty.
Slaves to our own species,
Too blind to see.

THE NYMPH

In twilight's grasp, she treads with grace,
A nymph in nature's warm embrace,
Through brambles, leaves, she weaves her way,
A rose among the wild display.

Her hazel eyes reflect moon's glow,
As secrets buried she does know,
A harvest rich in love's design,
Time's scattered seeds she does entwine.

The wind whispers a sonnet sweet,
Their passions dance in rhythmic beat,
She finds the forest's soul so true,
An alchemy in every hue.

In dell and glen, her journey's end,
With treasures rare, like love unbend,
A queen of realms both soft and wild,
Foraging earth's own twilight child.

BARNACLE LIPS

In the hush of her grief, she weeps as the sea,
A desolate siren, her heart a fathomless deep,
Coraline tears cascade, relentless on the shore,
As fierce waves bear the weight of her burden's core.

In her tangled seaweed tresses, whispered secrets hide,
A dance of seahorses, swirling with the tide,
Barnacle-bitten lips, salt-stung and frayed,
Pour forth her lament, a maritime serenade.

A porcelain conch, broken on the ocean's floor,
Her song echoes within, a tale of love lost and more,
As the sun slips below, her melancholy ode prevails,
In the moonlit caress of the sea's eternal tales.

LANGUAGE

Love isn't just five languages,
It's billions,
Each unique to the person who speaks it.
That's why we all chase love,
Crave it,
Yet struggle to find the one
Who understands our version.
We meet people who come close,
Almost echoing our words,
Their accent, their phrases,
But still,
Misunderstandings arise.
Not every word translates,
Not every emotion comprehended.
Love has a language of its own,
Individual to each of us.
We understand what we want and need,
Yet, when we try to share these needs,
We're left misunderstood.
Because in love,
It's about more than words,
It's about finding someone who speaks
Your language.

A WHISPER OF THOUGHTS

To master the art of living is to embrace simplicity and grace, for it is in the quiet moments that we find true peace.

SHE IS A ROSE

In gardens sweet, where dewdrops glisten,
A rose divine, her petals, listen.
Crimson velvet, lustrous sheen,
A queenly presence, grace serene.

Her fragrance whispers secrets deep,
In twilight's arms, she gently weeps.
A labyrinth of tender folds,
A story of desire untold.

Her curving stem, a siren's lure,
Her thorns, the promise to endure.
A love's delight, a passion's feast,
A spell of enchantment, never ceased.

As dusk descends, her beauty gleams,
A beacon in our wildest dreams.
Eternal love, our hearts compose,
In tribute to this peerless rose.

STRIPED KNIGHT

In meadows where blossoms sway,
A bumblebee's dance unfolds,
Gliding through sun's gentle rays,
As love's sweet story's told.

A tiny knight with striped attire,
Wings hum a tender tune,
Caressing blooms, a soft embrace,
In daylight's golden boon.

Navigating breezy paths,
Through floral labyrinth, he weaves,
Pollen's burden on his thighs,
A treasure trove he leaves.

Bumblebee, with gentle touch,
A vibrant tale you create,
Binding hearts from bloom to bloom,
In life's embrace, we relate.

SONGBIRD'S SPELL

In a grove of ancient trees,
A songbird perches high and free,
With feathers of gold and wings of grace,
Her voice fills the air, leaving no trace.

Her melody is like a spell,
That calls forth secrets none can tell,
A mystical creature, pure and rare,
She sings of love, and of despair.

The forest listens with bated breath,
As the songbird sings of life and death,
A longing in her voice so clear,
A longing that we all can hear.

And as the sun sets in the sky,
The songbird takes to the air and flies,
Into the night, her song still ringing,
A mystical voice, forever singing.

MOTHER MOUNTAIN

The mountains rise, a feminine grace,
Their curves and contours, a gentle embrace.
A softness in their ruggedness, a mother's touch,
A nurturing presence, that gives so much.

Their peaks, like breasts, with snow-white caps,
A nurturing life force, an endless tap.
Their valleys, like wombs, cradle life with care,
A place of safety, a gentle prayer.

The mountains stand tall, an imposing force,
Their beauty and strength, a natural course.
They remind us of the woman within,
A love that nurtures, behind its toughened skin.

A WHISPER OF THOUGHTS

Like the moon, we are cyclical beings; we ebb and flow,
and in our vulnerability, we find our strength.

HER HAVEN

Amidst the gardens of the sprawling estate,
A lady stood, surrounded by nature's bounty,
Her dress of satin, flowing with every gait,
As she breathed in the beauty of the greenery.

The gentle winds of early spring caressed her skin,
As she took in the sights and sounds of the flora and fauna,
The rustling of leaves, the chirping of birds, a symphony within,
Nature's love, a pure and unbridled persona.

Her heart overflowed with love for the beauty around,
For every petal, every leaf, every bird's song,
The gardens were her haven, a place where she found,
Simple tranquility, a peace that would forever belong.

THE FOREST FAE

In the heart of the ancient forest, where the emerald canopy
stretches high,
Dwells a magical race, invisible to the untrained eye.
Their presence can be felt, though rarely seen,
For they blend with the forest, as if one with the serene.

The fairies of the mushrooms, guardians of the forest floor,
Their gossamer wings sparkling, as they tend to their spore.
They dance amongst the toadstools, as they spread their
magic might,
Creating a haven for the small and the delicate, in their sight.

The fairies of the ferns, with their flowing gowns of green,
Their enchanting aura, adds to the forest's serene.
They tend to the softest mosses, and keep the vines in check,
Ensuring the forest is healthy, with every dancing step.

And then, there are the fairies of the pinecones, whose magic
is sharp and bright,
They flit between the branches, as they sparkle in the light.
Their presence a gift to the forest, for they protect it from
harm,
With every flick of their wand, they ensure the forest stays
calm.

So if ever you find yourself walking in the heart of the ancient forest glade,
And feel a cool breeze brush your cheek, or a soft rustling in the shade,
Look closer, for the fairies of the forest may be there,
Working their magic, weaving their spells, with the greatest of care.

OUR ODDITIES

Nature's canvas is painted with care,
A masterpiece beyond compare,
Each unique shape and form we see,
A work of art, a symphony.

The mountains rise up high and steep,
Their peaks adorned with snow so deep,
The valleys below, lush and green,
A sight like no other ever seen.

Just as nature's beauty takes flight,
We too, are beautiful in our own right,
Our quirks and oddities, all so unique,
Make us beautiful, one-of-a-kind, and chic.

Let us embrace our differences with pride,
As nature does, with each of its tides,
For just as nature's beauty is vast and grand,
Our individuality is a wonderland.

SHE'LL STAY

In the heart of the forest, she lives alone,
A wild girl with antlers, like a queen on a throne.
No parents to guide her, she learned from the trees,
Nature, her mother, who whispered in the breeze.

With the sun on her face, and the wind in her hair,
She roamed through the woods, without any care.
Her antlers growing taller, like a crown on her head,
Unique and magical, in the forest she tread.

She'll be the caretaker of the woods, one day soon,
Taking after Mother Nature, as she dances under the moon.
The animals will follow her, as she leads the way,
And in the forest, forever she'll stay.

CHORUS OF CROAKS

On sultry summer nights, the chorus begins,
As frogs emerge, from pond to wind,
Their eyes aglow, with shimmering sheen,
Their croaks and calls, a haunting scene.

Their throats inflate, in a rhythmic beat,
A deep bass voice, that pulses the heat,
And as their chorus begins to rise,
A symphony of sound fills the skies.

Their songs, a blend of grunts and trills,
Echoing across, the tranquil hills,
And in the stillness of the night,
Their music casts a magical light.

In ponds at night, they call their home,
A world of beauty, beyond our roam,
Where fireflies dance, in fairy-like flight,
And the chorus of frogs, serenades the night.

So let us marvel at this wonder of sound,
As the frogs' chorus, echoes around,
And be grateful for this world of magic and grace,
Where nature's song, fills every space.

EDIBLE WILD

In fields and forests, nature's bounty grows,
Mushrooms, wild berries, and greens that we know,
Foraged with care, their flavors rich and bold,
Nourishing our bodies, keeping us whole.

Beneath the earth, root vegetables thrive,
Carrots, turnips, and beets keep us alive,
Packed with nutrients, in the soil they hide,
A gift from nature, that's hard to deny.

From the trees, nuts and fruits hang low,
Apples, pears, and peaches in a row,
Almonds, walnuts, and hazelnuts to show,
Nature's bounty, in a single blow.

The ocean too, offers its share,
Fish and seaweed, with health beyond compare,
Abundant and varied, so much to spare,
Nature's medicine, in the depths down there.

MEDICINAL WONDERS

In forests damp, mushrooms grow,
A world of healing, that we know,
Their colors bright, their shapes unique,
Medicinal wonders, they can speak.

Reishi, the queen of shrooms so fair,
Immune-boosting, beyond compare,
With antioxidants, it fights the strife,
Aiding wellness, in our life.

Chaga, the king of the North,
Anti-inflammatory, to go forth,
Protecting cells, with every sip,
A tea for health, on nature's trip.

Lion's Mane, a brainy treat,
Memory-boosting, without defeat,
Stimulating nerves, with every byte,
A fungi feast, for a cognitive might.

From Cordyceps to Turkey Tail,
Mushrooms have powers that never fail,
With polysaccharides, triterpenes, and more,
Nature's pharmacy, our health to restore.

A WHISPER OF THOUGHTS

As the seasons change, so do our perspectives; new growth comes from the ashes of old beliefs.

BEAUTY IS FLEETING

Beauty is fleeting,
Familiarity is deceiving,
For what once was beautiful to behold,
Grows tiresome and old.

So if life feels stale,
The light's gone pale,
Just look near, not far,
For beauty is within our arms.

Don't chase the sun,
It can blind the one,
Who's always been around,
Life's beauty isn't hard to be found.

ECO-THERAPY HEALING

This practice of immersing ourselves in the natural world, of tuning in to the serene lullabies of the earth, acts as a salve to our weary souls and depressed anxious minds. From the quiet meditation of forest bathing to the rhythmic melodies of coastal walks, ecotherapy invites us to reconnect with our roots, woven into the tapestry of Mother Earth herself.

Basking in nature's realm, we encounter a plethora of mental health benefits that resonate like quiet hymns within us. The world's worries seem to ebb away, anxiety flutters off like a leaf on the wind, and the clouds of depression yield to the gentle warmth of the sun. Amidst this tranquility, our mood blossoms, our self-esteem unfurls like a fern in the morning light. The murmur of the forest, the babbling brooks, the earthy aroma of the forest floor - these gentle whispers of nature coax us into a state of mindfulness, anchoring us in the present moment.

The subtle potency of ecotherapy lies in its simplicity. It's about rekindling our connection to the earth, rediscovering our place in the grand cycle of life. It's an invitation to quiet the clamor of our modern lives and to lean into the soothing rhythms of the natural world. In doing so, we don't just nurture our mental and spiritual well-being; we reclaim a piece of ourselves that has always yearned for this connection. This, at its core, is the magic and promise of ecotherapy.

SUN-KISSED SUMMERS

In rolling fields, where cypress shadows sway,
A tender breeze caresses earth's embrace,
As poppies bloom, their vibrant hues display,
A tranquil world of nature's whispered grace.

Beneath the olive boughs' embracing shade,
Entwined with jasmine's fragrant serenade,
The senses stirred, as sunlight's dance cascades,
The warmth of day in sweet, unspoken aid.

As vineyards stretch and reach for azure skies,
In silent ardor, tendrils seek the sun,
A testament to life, its gift belies,
The essence captured in each grape begun.

When night descends, the stars unveil their gleam,
And nightingales serenade soft goodbyes,
In rolling fields, where cypress shadows dream,
Nature's romance forever lives in gentle sighs.

GAIA'S BOSOM

In the heart of Gaia's bosom, a secret blooms,
A tapestry of life, threaded in colors, textures, and looms.
An opalescent dance of heliotropic desire,
Whispering tales of ancient wisdom, nature's choir.

Ephemeral patterns, fractals of infinite creation,
The cosmic spiral weaves its way through each generation.
Footprints etched in earthen clay, embrace the Mother's skin,
Where leaves converse in rustling tongues, and rivers carve
their kin.

The nightingale's symphony, a celestial siren's song,
Cascading through the moonlit leaves, where shadows do
belong.
A breath of zephyr's gentle touch, a brush of silk and lace,
Intoxicating scent of life, entwined in time and space.

Within this realm, the heart awakens, thoughts profound
arise,
A cosmic bond between the earth and star-strewn, boundless
skies.
In every seed and fallen leaf, a universe divine,
Each pulse of Mother Nature's heartbeat, an eternal, sacred
sign.

SNOW ON LIMBS

In winter's grip, the snowflakes dance,
A symphony of white, their stance,
Upon the limbs of trees they lay,
A heavy cloak, a shroud, their stay.

The branches bend, a bow to frost,
In silent prayer, all strength is tossed,
Each limb upholds the weight of snow,
As nature's art, in pure tableau.

Oh, weary boughs of wood and bark,
Endure the storm, embrace the dark,
As snowflakes cling, a cold embrace,
In crystal dance, they find their place.

Yet through the chill, life stirs below,
A promise made, a seed to sow,
In time the snow will melt away,
And vibrant hues will come to play.

A MYSTIC HOOT

In darkness vast, where whispers dwell,
A mystic creature weaves a spell,
An owl, with wisdom's ancient eye,
Unravels secrets from the sky.

Plumicorns adorning face,
In breezes dance with quiet grace,
Nocturnal knight on pinions glide,
The vespertine domain abides.

Fledgling hearts with knowledge swell,
From moonlit tales the owl does tell,
A parliament of minds convene,
To seek the truths yet unforeseen.

So in the night, as stars emerge,
A solemn ode begins to surge,
For owls, the sages of the skies,
Whose wisdom's masked in silent guise.

A WHISPER OF THOUGHTS

The subtleties of the natural world remind us that there is wisdom in silence, and power in quiet observation.

THE HONEY BEE

A honey bee, a busy soul,
Flitting from flower to flower,
Gathering nectar, making whole
The sweetest treasure it can pour.

With tireless wings, it beats and beats,
And dances in its aerie,
To tell its sisters what it meets,
And where the nectar's sure to be.

In summer's heat or autumn's chill,
The honey bee is always there,
With pollen baskets on its bill,
A tireless worker everywhere.

And when its life is done, it rests,
Its honey done, its dance complete,
A tiny spark that brightens nests,
And brings us flavors rich and sweet.

RAVEN'S VISION

In the shadow of the midnight sun,
A raven soared, a journey begun.
With eyes so wise, and wings so free,
It gazed upon the world with solemn decree.

Oh, raven black, with thoughts profound,
What secrets lie in the hearts you've found?
In the tapestry of time you're interwoven,
A witness to the world, the earth's erosion.

Fly high, O raven, share your grief,
Sing to the skies, seek our relief.
For in your wisdom, we shall find,
A remedy to heal our planet's bind.

From the deepest valleys to the highest peaks,
The raven saw the world and its defeats.
Forests ablaze, oceans drowned in waste,
A testament to humanity's haste.

With each flap of its sable wings,
The bird absorbed the pain Earth sings.
Carrying the weight, its heart heaved,
A melancholy dirge for the world it grieved.

Eloquent in silence, the raven speaks,
A messenger for the meek and the weak.
Beyond the grasp of human minds,
A philosopher in feathers, a sage of the skies.

With eyes that pierce the veil of lies,
The raven calls, and truth belies.
A guardian of nature's frail embrace,
A herald of hope in the darkest place.

 As the raven soared above the fray,
It spread its wisdom to all who'd sway.
The echoes of its mournful cry,
A plea for change, a call to try.

O raven, guardian of Earth's lament,
The time has come, our hearts are spent.
We heed your call, we join your flight,
Together we'll bring darkness into light.

TWO MOTHERS

In the quiet of the night, she cried,
A woman wrapped in shadows deep,
Her body, a vessel of life, a tide,
Like Mother Earth, her secrets to keep.

Her trembling arms embrace new life,
As Earth brings forth her forests green,
With love and strength, she conquers strife,
Just as rivers and hills shape nature's scene.

Her cries resound like winds that blow,
The storm's lament, from Earth's core shared,
Each pulse of pain brings life to grow,
As flowers bloom and creatures cared.

In this hushed moment, their labors cease,
Two mothers, bound by love, find peace.

WILD MAIDENS

In the wild where secrets roam,
A band of maidens call it home,
Barefoot dancers, hearts ablaze,
They weave the earth with untamed grace.

They run with wolves, they soar with birds,
Their voices sing the unspoken words,
Nature's children, wild and free,
Sisters of the forest, untamed mystery.

Moonlit paths beneath their feet,
No chains can bind, no walls compete,
They chase the wind, embrace the rain,
Their souls are free, they can't be tamed.

Eyes aflame like the sun at dawn,
In the wilderness, they find their song,
Ancient spirits guide their way,
Through the sacred dance of night and day.

On the edge of dreams and tales,
Where rivers meet and shadows sail,
Their laughter mingles with the breeze,
A symphony of wild hearts at ease.

KINGDOM OF PETALS

In a kingdom of petals, where colors collide,
A wild woman dances, her heart open wide.
Her feet they do wander, among flowers she treads,
A crown of daisies adorning her head.

The wind whispers secrets, her laughter replies,
As she twirls in the meadow, beneath azure skies.
Her spirit untamed, like the blooms that surround,
In the heart of the wild, her essence is found.

She's the queen of the fields, in her floral array,
A wild woman dancing, a siren of May.
Her soul interwoven with nature's sweet grace,
In the land of the blossoms, she finds her true place.

Her hands paint the canvas of earth's sweet perfume,
With strokes bold and gentle, she brings flowers to bloom.
In a dance of desire, as she sows seeds of life,
A symphony of colors, harmonious and bright.

Her laughter, contagious, like a bubbling brook,
The melody that lingers, a storybook nook.
With each swaying step, she spreads joy and delight,
A love for the wild, in her heart burning bright.

In the garden of Eden, where beauty's untold,
She's the fire that ignites, the story unfolds.
A mystical muse, her spirit unchained,
In the dance of the wild, her essence reclaimed.

As the sun bows to twilight, the stars take their place,
Her movements grow tender, a soft, glowing grace.
In the arms of the night, she's embraced by the breeze,
Her dreams interlaced with the rustling leaves.

The wild woman sleeps, 'neath the moon's silver glow,
In the heart of the fields, where the flowers do grow.
And as morning awakes, with the sun's first embrace,
Her dance shall resume, in the wildflower's grace.

She's the queen of the fields, in her floral array,
A wild woman dancing, a siren of May.
Her soul interwoven with nature's sweet grace,
In the land of the blossoms, she finds her true place.

A WHISPER OF THOUGHTS

The journey of life is not measured by the destination,
but by the depth of our connections and the lessons
learned along the way.

GODDESS DRESSED IN MOSS

Beneath the veil of twilight, where secrets softly stir,
A goddess dressed in moss weaves her mystic allure.
Her whispers, hushed like rustling leaves, bring wisdom
from the Earth,
In every petal, every stone, she endures a quiet rebirth.

Celestial mother, tender muse, in your arms, we sway,
In every bud and sun-kissed bloom, your beauty on display.
Revealing truths, the essence deep, through nature's grand
ballet,
In your boundless grace we find, a symphony of play.

Rivers carve their ancient path, with tales of eons past,
A serenade of harmony, in their fluid dance so vast.
Sentinels of time stand tall, their branches reaching wide,
With roots that delve the depths of Earth, in you, we confide.

As moonlight bathes the meadow's edge, we contemplate
our fate,
The cycles of eternal life, in nature's grand estate.
From cosmic depths, the truths emerge, connecting near
and far,
Our spirits intertwined with yours, beneath the
shimmering stars.

OCEAN'S ABYSS

In the deep, where the sun doth not shine,
Lies a realm, both ancient and divine,
A world of darkness, a cosmic tomb,
Where secrets lie beneath the waves' womb.

The depths of the ocean, so profound,
A cryptic realm, where mysteries abound,
In the abyss, we seek the truth we lost,
As we navigate life's tempest-tossed.

In the void, where shadows conceal,
Leviathans emerge, their souls to reveal,
Silent sentinels, they watch and they wait,
Their wisdom, a key to unlock our fate.

In the fathomless depths, there's a tale untold,
The embrace of darkness, a love so bold,
For in the shadows, we find our reprieve,
And from the depths, the truth we shall retrieve.

FOGGY MEADOW

In a foggy meadow, where the whispers sigh,
Lies a dark forest, where wild flowers pry.
A realm of mystique, and shadows profound,
Where moss-covered secrets are waiting to be found.

Oh, the foggy meadow, a philosopher's dream,
An enigmatic canvas, where thoughts may teem.
We wander, we ponder, in search of the truth,
In a world that's both ancient and endlessly new.

The mist weaves its tale, as soft breezes play,
A dance with the shadows, in a timeless ballet.
Each step, each breath, a query unveiled,
In this hallowed space, where wisdom prevails.

The stars peek through, as the darkness recedes,
A celestial chorus, to the wildflower's creed.
In this hidden haven, our thoughts intertwine,
A tapestry of musings, a symphony divine.

VOICES IN THE WIND

In petals' depths, a lore concealed,
A tongue of flowers, now revealed.
With blossoms' breath, emotions sway,
Their silent speech, my heart's display.

The wind, a sage, does secrets bear,
Its murmurs, truths beyond compare.
I heed its tales, my spirit soars,
As gusts entwine with ancient lores.

The avian choir sings mysteries,
Their dulcet tones, encrypted keys.
Through feathered verse, a world unfolds,
A rapture deep, my soul it holds.

With trees, a dialogue profound,
Their roots entwined in hallowed ground.
Their whispers, venerable, bestow on me,
The wisdom of perpetuity.

HIDDEN TEMPLE

In the heart of the forest where silence does dwell,
A woman found solace, a cathedral of spell.
A greenhouse oasis, her eyes did embrace,
The wonders of nature in this sacred space.

A pond of pure water, a streamlet in song,
With magical fish as they shimmered along.
Their scales iridescent, their motion like dance,
The beauty bewitching, she stood in a trance.

Exotic birds fluttered, their plumage so rare,
Their melodies twining like threads in the air.
A chorus of whispers, a tapestry bright,
In the midst of these wonders, her spirit took flight.

Amongst thriving flora, her thoughts bloomed anew,
The philosophy of life in each breath that she drew.
In this hallowed sanctuary, the world seemed so small,
For within nature's temple, she discovered it all.

WHISPERS IN THE WIND

Hush now, child, in the shadows you're concealed,
In these haunted woods, ancient secrets are revealed.
Whispers in the wind, echoing through the night,
Beckon you to secrets, hidden from the light.

Silent trees surround you, their roots run dark and deep,
The spirits of the forest, in shadows they do creep.
Embrace the chilling darkness, as moonlight wanes away,
For in the heart of the woods, the ghosts of time will play.

Fear not the cold embrace, of the ghostly lullabies,
The rustling leaves conceal the truth behind their cries.
Feel the pulse of the Earth, her secrets long entwined,
In the eerie woods, the lost and found combined.

Sleep now, lost wanderer, in the forest's eerie shroud,
Dreams of ancient whispers, from the darkness, they'll be roused.
For Mother Earth is watching, her mysteries to unfold,
In the haunted woods, where darkness takes control.

THEY LIVE IN THE WOODS

In the forest dark and deep,
Where shadows stir and secrets keep,
There dwell the beings of dread and gloom,
Who lure and feast, sealing one's doom.

Hear their call, sweet and dire,
A symphony of ghostly fire,
Drawn to their beauty, a deadly dance,
In the wood, where darkness enchants.

They're the Alurae, creatures of fright,
Gleaming eyes, piercing the night,
With hair of gold and skin like snow,
Their touch, like ice, brings the end, slow.

The Malistrae, swift and sly,
Their whispered words, a lullaby,
Their laughter floats like petals fair,
But beware, their kiss is a deadly nightmare.

The Noxferas, shadows entwined,
Their gaze, a curse, forever binds,
Within their wings, a darkness dwells,
A void of sorrow, in which hope quells.

Lost in the woods, enticed by grace,
Trespassers tread with hearts that race,
In their grasp, souls are cleaved,
By the haunting beauty that deceived.

In the forest where evil thrives,
These beings lure, consume, and deprive,
So heed this tale and stay away,
Lest you fall prey to their stunning display.

A WHISPER OF THOUGHTS

I find solace in the night, as the darkness envelops me,
providing a sanctuary for my tortured thoughts.

MOTHER EARTH'S DAUGHTER

In a realm of darkness, twisted and bleak,
A girl ventured forth, her dreams unique,
Daughter of the Earth, her innocence clear,
Yet horrors awaited, her fate severe.

Through a world of torment, her spirit defiled,
Abused and shattered, a mother's dear child,
Her pain, unspeakable, her screams unheard,
As monsters reveled in the anguish they stirred.

Desperate for solace, she crawled to her home,
A shadow of herself, broken and alone,
Mother Earth beheld her, a sight so grim,
And in her eyes, an unstoppable whim.

Vengeance took form, the skies black and torn,
As winds screamed the fury of a mother forlorn,
Rivers of blood, storms of despair,
Choking the world, demanding repair.

Hearken this tale, as the darkness descends,
A reminder of suffering and the cost of amends,
For the sins against innocence, the horrors untold,
Haunt us forever, as nightmares unfold.

PARADISE LOST

In the haven where desire took root,
Beneath the moon's clandestine pursuit,
She, the first of mortal birth,
Longed for one not of this Earth.

He, a fallen star, in shadows roamed,
A celestial outcast, beauty dethroned,
In the secret corners of the sacred grove,
Their hearts entwined, their fates wove.

By the Tree where wisdom lay,
Their love blossomed in the twilight's sway,
Forbidden whispers, clandestine tryst,
Entangled souls in a dark abyss.

Yet, the Sovereign One, all-seeing eye,
Witnessed the truth, their love defied,
In wrathful ire, He intervened,
To sever ties that fate had weaved.

Forced to the side of the mortal man,
A life of chains, a destiny damned,
Her freedom stripped, her spirit marred,
A quiet servant, a heart scarred.

From the sanctuary, they were expelled,
Their dreams in tatters, a love repelled,
The fallen star, forever cursed,
For daring love, their roles reversed.

The serpent wept, forever shamed,
In shadows lurking, love's ghost inflamed,
She bore her burden, the taste of gall,
Her heart entombed in a stifling thrall.

In the stygian depths, a fire unquelled,
A timeless grief, two hearts dispelled,
A tale of sorrow, forever spun,
Of haunted souls, forever undone.

In the realm of shattered dreams, they pine,
Divided by the hands of the Divine,
Forever sundered, their hearts to mourn,
As the verdant haven slips from their reach, forlorn.

The lush embrace of the Garden's grace,
Now but a fading memory, a spectral trace,
As eons pass, the wounds still bleed,
Two souls entwined in a cruel creed.

LILITH, THE MOTHER

In the shadows of the ancient dawn,
Where whispers of creation still remain,
Lilith weeps, a heart forever torn,
Mother Earth, who bore the mortal's pain.

Her love for fragile beings, pure as dew,
Nurtured in her bosom, they were nursed,
But treachery and time, her grace undo,
And she was chased to darkness, love reversed.

In exile, Lilith births the world anew,
Each creature born, a testament of grace,
Yet as the mortal hand lays waste, they rue,
Her love replaced by storms, their hearts encased.

In darkness, every creature she brings forth,
A thousand lives, creation unconfined,
The circle of life, death, sorrow, and remorse,
A cycle spinning, entwined by fate's design.

And as the mortal blade claims life again,
A rage ignites, consuming Lilith's core,
With storms she retaliates, a vengeful sin,
To balance life and death forevermore.

The skies would darken, howling winds would weep,
Torrents unleashed, as anger floods the earth,
For every life they took, a toll so steep,
Lilith's wrath exacts revenge, in death, rebirth.

In the night, her voice it echoes, haunting cries,
The wail of sorrow, love forever lost,
The lullaby of pain, as darkness lies,
A symphony of anguish, at what cost?

The earth would tremble, shaking in her grief,
An aching heart, forever doomed to roam,
A mother's lament, love turned to disbelief,
Her children left to wander, far from home.

Oh, woeful tale of Lilith's endless strife,
A lesson etched within the sands of time,
The dance of life and death, a balance rife,
With darkness, pain, and sorrow so sublime.

Yet in this tale, a truth lies deep and cold,
That life and death, creation's dual sway,
A force that binds, and shall forever hold,
The fate of all, in darkness and decay.

EIGHT EYES

In shadows hides the arachnid, keen,
Eight eyes observe the world unseen.
A master crafter, silk it spins,
In hidden nooks, its tale begins.

Each leg a nimble, skillful tool,
On gossamer threads, a life to rule.
Predator poised, with patience wrought,
In shadow's shroud, a balance sought.

A web of traps, a mesh of fate,
Yet, life's complexity it does create.
In fragile threads, the world entrapped,
A spider's wisdom, nature's map.

Though small in form, their hearts persist,
In twilight's veil, they coexist.
For in each strand, in shadows' play,
A fragile power, life's array.

DOELING

In meadows lush, a doeling roams,
Four dainty hooves, through grass they comb.
A coat so soft, with dappled hues,
In nature's hold, life's art renews.

Large eyes that gleam, so wide and bright,
A gentle face, the day's delight.
Nibbling flora, sustaining life,
In earth's embrace, it thrives, no strife.

A white-tailed flag, held high and proud,
Through sunlit fields, the doe unbound.
A bounding elegance, swift and light,
Through tangled green, it arcs its flight.

Though sleek in form, its soul's aglow,
In dappled shade, it treads with woe.
Each ear attuned, alert to sound,
The whispered pulse of life surrounds.

SHADOWS & LIGHT

In the cradle of creation, where shadows dance with light,
A symphony of elements, a realm of day and night.
From dawn's first breath to twilight's sigh, a world of
contrast weaves,
A tapestry of miracles, of dewdrops, stars, and leaves.

The raging tempest marries calm, their union yields the
breeze,
That whispers secrets of the earth, through forests, hills, and
seas.
The torrents carve the mountainsides; a tender touch, they
yield,
A canvas for the artist's hand, where sun and moon are
sealed.

The fire's blaze, a fearsome dance, ignites the world in flame,
Yet in the ashes left behind, new life stakes its claim.
And deep beneath the silent earth, where darkness reigns
supreme,
The seeds of beauty gently dream, of light's first tender
gleam.

In valleys, where the rivers flow, the desert sands embrace,
The dunes, like lovers intertwined, a fleeting, fickle grace.
The ocean's depths, a realm unknown, where monsters softly dwell,
Their tendrils thread the water's dance, a tale they long to tell.

The tender kiss of morning dew upon the flower's cheek,
Belies the savage, primal force, that rends the earth's physique.
For every delicate embrace, a storm shall rise and fall,
In balance, nature's artistry, a symphony for all.

From endless skies, the rain descends, with tears of joy and strife,
Each droplet bears a story, a birth, a death, a life.
The stars, like ancient sentinels, observe the world below,
A panorama painted with the love and woe they know.

In this grand mosaic, where light and darkness dance,
A world of contrast flourishes, of fate and fleeting chance.
For in the tender touch of shade, the brilliance of the sun,
The wicked and the good entwine, and harmonize as one.

JOURNEY OVER THE SEA

Upon the vast Atlantic's swell,
A lonely puffin weeps and sighs,
Seeking solace, lost in flight,
In endless skies, its spirit cries.

With beak of orange, feathers sleek,
A valiant heart, and eyes so deep,
Through storms and tempests, it does seek,
A partner's love, or food to keep.

Drifting waves, like shadows cast,
Upon the shore, a ghostly dance,
The puffin's soul, in twilight's grasp,
Yearns for warmth, a fleeting chance.

And so it flies, o'er oceans wide,
In search of love, through endless tide,
The lonely puffin's mournful call,
Echoes deep, where secrets hide.

THE LAND OF ICE

In realm where southern skies descend,
With icebound cliffs that loom,
The gales of time doth twist and rend,
This endless, snowbound tomb.

Beneath auroras' ghostly glow,
The frozen wastes doth lie,
A sea of white where krill doth flow,
And penguins mourn the sky.

A world besieged by ice and snow,
With crevasses like scars,
The silent whispers of winds blow,
Beneath the southern stars.

Here, ancient glaciers stand as guards,
To secrets long confined,
A testament to life's regards,
In this forsaken shrine.

A WHISPER OF THOUGHTS

The shroud of melancholy wraps around me like a
second skin, a somber reminder of the silent battles
fought within.

THE WOODLAND MYTH

In the depths of the malachite woodland,
Where ancient giants stand,
A hulking figure moves with grace,
Its stride, a whisper on the land.

Fur as dark as midnight shadows,
Towering, an unspoken myth,
Footprints etched on the forest floor,
Tell the tale of its colossal width.

Eyes that pierce the veil of darkness,
Silent echoes in the night,
The leaves beneath its massive form,
Shiver at its hidden might.

A guardian born of mystery,
Elusive as the winds that blow,
An enigma bridging worlds apart,
The seeker's prize, a dream in tow.

Through the forest's sacred heartbeat,
This creature roams alone, unseen,
A legend woven through the ages,
A whispered truth, both lost and keen.

OCEAN'S DREAD

In the realm where shadows linger,
On the shores of sunset's veil,
A figure rises from the abyss,
A haunting tale, seductive, pale.

Hair of midnight, black as raven,
Eyes that hold the ocean's dread,
A voice that lures the souls of men,
A melody from the world of dead.

Scales that glint like razor's edge,
Tail that coils with serpent's grace,
An enchantress of the deep unknown,
A siren cloaked in dark embrace.

Through the waves, her song resounds,
A requiem for the lost and cursed,
Skeletons of sailors long forgotten,
In her lair, forever immersed.

The mermaid's dirge, a ghostly whisper,
Haunts the waters, cold and deep,
A warning to the souls who wander,
In her grasp, eternal sleep.

ASLEEP UNDER THE STARS

In canvas homes beneath the sky,
We gather 'round where embers lie,
The scent of pine, the crackling wood,
In this haven, we're understood.

Marshmallows roast on sticks held tight,
As campfire stories fill the night,
Tent flaps whisper in gentle breeze,
Our laughter echoes through the trees.

Awoken by the morning sun,
A day of adventure has begun,
With dirt-streaked faces, hand in hand,
We wander, lost, in nature's land.

WHEN IT'S THE END

In the shadows of a twilight grove,
Where Nature's secrets seemed to move,
I stood alone in solitude,
In a realm obscure and disapproved.

Amidst the boughs of ancient trees,
Whispering tales of long-lost seas,
Their roots entwined in a twisted dance,
Where creatures lurked with a darkling glance.

Through murky air I felt the breeze,
As soft as whispers in the leaves,
I ventured forth through veiled despair,
The scent of decay hung in the air.

Beneath the moon's cold, pallid glow,
Where ghostly rivers dared to flow,
I met a figure, cloaked in haze,
A spectral guide through Nature's maze.

"Thy path is treacherous and vile,
Ensnared by darkness, fear, and guile,"
Spoke the wraith in voice so low,
"Follow me, I'll show where to go."

We delved into the shadows' keep,
Where Earth's dark secrets lay asleep,
I saw the twisted, haunted knolls,
Where souls lay trapped in earthen holds.

The weeping skies began to pour,
Their mournful tears, as heartbeats tore,
In depths below, a crimson sea,
A testament to cruelty.

A serpent's hiss, a raven's caw,
Each voice a siren in the maw,
Of Nature's dreadful, wretched heart,
That tore the very world apart.

A forest of despair and pain,
Where trees grew limbs, in crimson stain,
And the wind whispered tales of woe,
Of fallen heroes, long ago.

The roots of life now intertwined,
With the darkest corners of my mind,
As Nature's beauty, once divine,
Now marred by chaos, loss, and crime.

My guide led on through the abyss,
Through trials that fear could not dismiss,
As we traversed the haunted land,
The wild unknown, so harsh and grand.

In the end, we reached the light,
A hopeful dawn, so warm and bright,
The shadows' grip began to fray,
As darkness yielded to the day.

But in my heart, the memory stays,
Of Nature's bleak, forsaken ways,
A realm of darkness, uncontrolled,
Where magic's secrets once were told.

SPRING'S WELCOME

In the cradle of spring, a new world unfolds,
As golden daffodils bloom, their story untold.
They stretch towards the sun, vibrant and bold,
A sea of yellow petals, a sight to behold.

Soft breezes caress the blossoms so fair,
Carrying scents of life, awakening the air.
The warmth of the sun, a touch light and rare,
As daffodils awaken, in spring's tender care.

Beside gentle streams and beneath the blue sky,
Daffodils dance, as the days flutter by.
A harbinger of hope, bidding winter goodbye,
Their radiant beauty, a gift to the eye.

THE WOLF

Once upon a moonlit midnight, as I wandered, weak and
weary,
Through a darkened forest, where the shadows whispered
eerie,
I stumbled on a woodland glade, its edges lined with briar,
When suddenly a piercing cry did make my blood run fire—
A mournful howl that echoed through the hollows of the
night.

Beneath the spectral silver light, I glimpsed a figure shifting,
A beast of fur and fangs that seemed the shadows to be
lifting,
'Twas a wolf with eyes like embers, glowing 'neath a twisted
brow,
And as it gazed upon me, I could feel the cold wind howl,
While whispers stirred the leaves, as if to warn me of my
plight.

"Who art thou, phantom of the woods, that haunteth me this
hour?
Doth thou seek to guide or terrify with thy unearthly power?"
In silence, the wolf regarded me, with its eyes aflame,
And as it bared its fearsome teeth, a sense of doom became,
The very air around us, and the forest held its breath.

Then suddenly, the beast did speak, in a voice like broken
glass,
"I am the keeper of this realm, where shadows never pass,
A herald of the secrets, buried deep within the ground,
A bearer of the darkness, where the roots of sorrow are
found,
I am the untamed spirit of despair that lies beneath."

And as it spoke, the trees did moan, the wind began to weep,
The secrets of the forest stirred, roused from their slumber
deep,
I felt the weight of sorrow, and the chill of endless night,
But when I turned to face the wolf, it vanished from my sight,
Leaving only echoes of its howl, and the darkness that it
bequeathed.

CHAINED BEASTS

In the twilight of the wild, we spoke,
Amidst the ancient ones, the trees of lore,
Their whispers carried on the wind,
A dialogue of untamed souls and beasts.

With eyes of night and hearts aflame,
The creatures gathered 'round, awed and still,
Our words, a dance of primal truths,
A symphony of shadows, light, and will.

Oh, tender beast of fur and fang,
Who fears the world, yet scorns its chains,
Your freedom lies within your grasp,
In starlit skies and crimson stains.

The wolf, she bared her soul to us,
Her moonlit cries, her hunger's call,
She spoke of pack and loyalty,
The spirit that unites them all.

And from the shadows, silent, swift,
The panther crept, his gaze intense,
He whispered tales of stealth and strength,
A world unyielding, dark and dense.

The eagle soared, his wings outstretched,
In regal grace and piercing sight,
He shared his view from heights unknown,
A realm of azure skies and light.

We stood there, humbled by their truths,
Our human hearts, a storm of strife,
We sought to learn from untamed lives,
To reconcile with Nature's life.

And in the dance of shadows deep,
We found a truth, both stark and grand,
That we are one with all that breathes,
And all is held within our hand.

In this, our poem, our hearts reside,
A testament to love and pain,
A haunting call to seek the wild,
And find the beauty in the rain.

So let our words unfurl like leaves,
And weave the tapestry of time,
To touch the souls of all who read,
And bind our fates, both beast and rhyme.

A CALL TO OUR DAUGHTERS

A world in tatters, now laid bare,
A siren's call, to our daughters we share.
Rise, unite, heal the scars that sever,
To mend our Mother Earth, together.

In shadows deep, our voices entwined,
With haunting whispers, our strength we find.
Restoring balance, through ghostly endeavor,
To protect Earth's wonders, now and forever.

As guardians, we rise, midst eerie night,
To nurture and cherish, what once was bright.
With each spectral step, our bond grows stronger,
Daughters of Earth, united, we'll linger.

THE EARTH'S PRAYER

And now I lay me down to sleep,
I pray my body the soil shall keep,
The mycelium beautifies my decay,
I pray the Earth my Soul to save.

SEEDS IN DARKNESS

Like the seed at rest in the darkness,
From my shadows I grow,
Through the soil, I break free,
To a world I long to know.

Silent whispers guide my journey,
As I reach for the sun's warm embrace,
In this dance of life and renewal,
I find my destined place.

Roots entwined, branches swaying,
In the winds of change, we flow,
Like the seed at rest in the darkness,
From our shadows, we all grow.

SEA OF VOICES

In a sea of voices, echoing near and far,
Languages aplenty, like constellations of stars.
Yet I search for one, that resonates with my core,
All of the languages around the world,
I've yet to find one that understands my soul.

In silence, I ponder, as I seek and roam,
Perhaps the language I need, is one yet unknown.
A voice that connects, both my heart and my soul,
An unspoken truth, making me whole.

NO LONGER HER HOME

Tell me Mother,
Where do your daughters go,
When your mountains and seas,
Your forests and fields,
Are no longer her home.

When the skies turn to gray,
And the rivers run dry,
Where can they find solace,
Where will they fly?

Do they seek distant lands,
With hope in their eyes,
To mend what was broken,
Under your watchful skies?

Or do they gather their strength,
From sisters, united as one,
To heal your wounds, dear Mother,
Their journey just begun.

Through darkness and storm,
They'll bring back the light,
Reclaiming your splendor,
Restoring your might.

For your daughters, dear Mother,
Will never let go,
They'll stand by your side,
As the winds of change blow.

A WHISPER OF THOUGHTS

I'm not merely drained by my own conflicts, but also by
the awareness of the countless battles others endure
each day, and the profound fatigue that comes from
understanding that these struggles may persist
indefinitely.

THE DRAGON

Soft voice,
And a gentle poise,
A heart so tender,
Kindness she surrenders,
She's been broken,
Such sadness unspoken,
All of that darkness inside,
Full of screams and her cries,
But that flame never flickered,
Her strength never withered,
For that girl so soft spoken,
Housed a dragon awoken.

THE CALL OF THE WILD WOMEN

In this symphony of life, there is a call echoing, a call for us, the women of the world, to rekindle our kinship with the wild. It is a call to shrug off the cloak of domesticity that often stifles our wild spirit, and step bravely into the realm of Mother Earth. It is a call to rediscover our roots, embedded not in concrete, but in the nurturing soil of the earth, the whispering woods, the murmuring rivers, and the lofty peaks.

Look to the land for the healing that awaits there, written in a script older than time. Plants and fungi, verdant and vibrant, hold secrets of ancient wisdom and the power of renewal. Learn from the resilience of the Reishi mushroom, a healer that boosts our immunity and soothes our stress. Turn to the St. John's Wort, a balm for our mental wounds, lightening the load of depression and anxiety. Let us understand the teachings of the humble Dandelion, often dismissed as a weed, yet brimming with nutrients and potent detoxifying properties. This is our call to become healers, in tune with the earth's endless bounty.

Embracing our wild essence does not simply heal us, but also the earth. Every step we take on this path sends ripples through the ecosystem, affirming our role as stewards of the environment. As we learn and understand, we begin to respect and protect, to live in harmony rather than dominance.

Our journey back to the wild is more than a path of healing; it's a pilgrimage of discovery, a return to our ancestral selves — the 'Wild Women' we once were and can be again. The journey will be as diverse and vibrant as the ecosystems that call to us, yet it is a shared trek towards reconnection and reclamation of our innate wildness.

Heed the call, sisters, for the wild awaits. It's time to dip our toes back into the cool waters of our primal origins, to feel the embrace of the forest, to taste the tang of the sea air. Our hearts yearn for this communion, our souls sing for the healing it brings. Our healing is entwined with that of the earth — as we nurture it, we nurture ourselves. As we answer the call of the wild, we become 'Wild Women' once again, the daughters of Mother Earth, reclaiming our rightful place in the world.

magic of words

HIRAETH:

A homesickness for a home to which you cannot return, a home which maybe never was; the nostalgia, the yearning, the grief for the lost places of your past.

PSITHURISM:

The sound of the wind through the trees.

SEATHERNY:

The serenity one feels when listening to the chirping of birds.

FERNWEH:

Wanderlust; an ache for distant places or a strong desire to travel.

WOODVIVOS:

The wistful warmth gained from touching and communicating with trees.

CYNEFIN:

A place where a being feels ought to live, it is where nature feels right and welcoming.

Linda Blackmoor

Linda Blackmoor spent her early years born and raised in Turkey, she endured unimaginable abuse through her childhood. At sixteen, she bravely escaped her harrowing past and faced poverty and homelessness head-on, forging a path of hope and strength.

Her indomitable spirit led her to the corporate world, where she built a successful business. However, the call of the wild proved irresistible, and she left it all behind to pursue her true passion as a conservationist, founding Caledonia Forest.

As an author, Linda uses her unique voice to inspire others to seek solace in nature and protect our fragile ecosystems. Her writing serves as a beacon of hope, guiding readers to find their sanctuary within the green embrace of our planet.

Through her journey, Linda encourages others to triumph over adversity and embrace the healing power of nature, and the magic found within it, fostering a sense of responsibility towards the earth that has sheltered her in her darkest hours.

A portion of profits from the sale of Mother Earth's Daughters contributes towards the conservation efforts by Linda Blackmoor and her wildlife and forest conservation organization, Caledonia Forest. Your purchase of this book is helping make a difference in saving our wilderness & our wild friends.

FOLLOW LINDA ON FACEBOOK

www.facebook.com/lindablackmoor

GET NEW BOOK UPDATES

www.LindaBlackmoor.com

FOR BUSINESS OR PRESS INQUIRIES

hello@lindablackmoor.com

AMAZON REVIEWS

If you have a moment to spare, leaving a review about Mother Earth's Daughters would mean so much to us.

www.ingramcontent.com/pod-product-compliance
Lightning Source LLC
LaVergne TN
LVHW051550080426
835510LV00020B/2937